Criminal Justice
Through the Looking Glass

Everything You Need to Know That Your Lawyer Won't Tell You

A Step-by-Step Guide to Surviving Jail and Prison from Arrest Through Appeals

Daniel Teitelbaum, PhD

Here's what readers are saying:

5 out of 5 stars I hope you never need the information in this important book. *"I could not put this book down. The author paints a very dire picture of the Kafkaesque situation for defendants. Those of us on the outside believe that the Constitution affords us due process and equal protection under the law. But for many who end up in "the system" there is very little hope of mounting a vigorous defense, or of successfully appealing, even if you go bankrupt to pay a lawyer."*

***

5 out of 5 stars Insightful and Important. A must read! *"It is an eye-opening inside view into the US criminal justice system. There are a lot of misconceptions into how things really work, and this is a step-by-step manual of its inner workings. If you are ever in the situation of the author this will give you a good starting point to help avoid mistakes that could cost you your freedom, sanity and potentially bankrupt you and your family."*

***

5 out of 5 stars A Remarkable Book. *"To call it eye-opening is an understatement. It is a sobering indictment of the judicial system. Teitelbaum makes a powerful, convincing case about the collusion and power structure among defense lawyers, prosecutors, and judges that act to the detriment of the innocent. His case for the innocent taking a plea deal rather than going to trial is grievously convincing, based on the overwhelming likelihood of conviction and severe sentencing, and because a trial is too much of a hassle for everyone but the innocent. It is a terribly depressing book. But it is a brilliant, eloquent, extremely readable, disheartening, convincing indictment of "our" judicial system, and our fantasy of innocent until proven guilty."*

Dedication

To the memory of Jacob Teitelbaum, 2005 – 2024.

Acknowledgments

I am deeply grateful to Dr. Michelle Rondon for all her help in getting this book published. I couldn't have done it without you.

Author's and publisher's note:

Copyright © 2025 by Daniel Teitelbaum

ISBN: 979-8-9944811-0-3

Published in Vienna, Virginia

Contents

Preface

Most criminal defendants discover too late that nobody in the courtroom is defending them. The prosecutors attack them, focusing entirely on evidence of guilt and ignoring all evidence of innocence. They believe the judge will be a neutral, disinterested arbiter and are surprised when he behaves as if he is in cahoots with the prosecutor. And the defense attorney's job is to pretend to be the defendant's friend while trying to convince him to take whatever plea-deal the prosecutor is offering. The whole process has devolved into an embarrassing pantomime designed to fool the defendant into believing that his rights are being defended.

Spend a few hours in any prison law library and you are certain to see inmates fighting to right the wrongs that were done to them by the courts. These inmates can be divided into two groups: hoary veterans with the thousand-yard stare grimly searching the legal databases and typing up motions, and rookies, shuffling about with the deer-in-the-headlights stare asking the law clerks how to begin.

Eavesdrop on their conversations and you will hear the rookies say, "But I didn't know any of that...." and the law clerks saying, "Unfortunately, now it's too late..."

In the law, you really only get one chance. If your lawyer fails to object when your rights are violated, you can't appeal later. You'll run into things called the "Plain Error Standard" and the "Contemporaneous Objection Rule," both of which make winning on appeal effectively impossible. If your lawyer does not defend you vigorously or fails to raise arguments that you are sure would win, you won't be able to make those arguments later. Instead, you'll have to try to prove that you received ineffective assistance of counsel, which is also nearly impossible.

Tantalus, a son of Zeus, was punished in the underworld by being afflicted with a raging thirst. He was placed in a lake whose waters receded every time he bent down to take a drink. Convicted felons, likewise, can see how they've been hoodwinked only after it becomes too late to do anything about it.

The people who need the information the most - the accused, the indicted and the convicted - are precisely the people who don't have it until it is too late. So that is the need that this book proposes to fill: get the necessary information to the appropriate people before, rather than after, they need it.

The primary audience for this book is the accused themselves, anybody that has just been arrested. Most have no idea what to expect.

The secondary audience is friends and family of the accused. Many would like to be of help but have no idea how to go about it. They don't know anything about the law. They don't know anything about trials or plea bargains. They don't know how long the process should take and they don't know how much it will all cost. They feel helpless, and helplessness is a miserable feeling. They need a book that breaks the whole process down step by step and lets them know how they can contribute.

And then there is everybody else. Most people wonder what it would be like to wake up in jail, to be cross-examined by prosecutor in front of a jury, or to do time in prison. Would they know what to do? Could they win? Would they survive?

Stories about prisoners have been favorites for centuries, from "The Count of Monte Christo" to "Les Misérables" to "Cool Hand Luke" and "The Shawshank Redemption."

Nationwide, criticism of the costly and overcrowded prison system is only growing, as is anger over soaring incarceration rates. More than a million people are convicted of felonies each year. The total number of appeals annually is around 70,000.

People do not understand what the American criminal justice system has become. People believe that it is designed to convict the guilty and exonerate the innocent. Nope. The system is designed to convict everybody, innocent and guilty alike. Its goal is to force every defendant to accept a plea bargain. Those that have the temerity to refuse to plead guilty and insist on going to trial are taught a lesson by being given an unfair trial followed by a harsh sentence.

The laws and rules of court were written by lawyers for the benefit of lawyers. In the field of economics, workers are generally presumed to want to make as much money as possible while doing as little work as possible. Put another way, workers have two objectives: maximize pay, minimize work. In the criminal justice system, lawyers accomplish these objectives by charging clients as much money as possible and then convincing them to plead guilty. Trials are expensive and time-consuming and must therefore be avoided.

It is instructive to look at the incentive structure for prosecutors. Are prosecutors rewarded for giving shorter sentences? Are they rewarded for going to trial? Are they rewarded for exonerating the innocent? The answer to all three questions is no. They are rewarded for convictions and long prison sentences.

Long sentences and heavy penalties benefit prosecutors because they allow them to apply more pressure on defendants and force more plea deals. Plea deals, by eliminating trials, reduce work and increase throughput, so they're good for judges and defense attorneys, too.

But, for some reason, prosecutors and judges are ashamed of this. They prefer to maintain the pious fiction that everyone in America has a right to a fair trial by a jury of their peers. In order to conceal the truth, they dissemble; they lie. And these are not victimless lies. The millions of people churning though our courts, jails, and prisons are wasting their life's savings fighting cases that they do not realize cannot be won, and then are sentenced to prison for decades.

Simply put, it's not a fair fight. It pains me to watch the strong (i.e., lawyers and judges) take advantage of the weak (e.g,. defendants, appellants, and their families.) It is as offensive as watching three big fifth graders bully a second grader on the schoolyard. What this book aims to do is give the little kid some boxing lessons - give him a few skills with which to fight back, all in the interest of fairness.

There are many books critical of the criminal-justice system. Most are written by lawyers, a few by academics and journalists. They have titles like "The New Jim Crow," (M. Alexander) "Mistrial: An Inside Look at how the Criminal Justice System Works ... and Sometimes Doesn't," (M. Geragos & P. Harris), and "Charged: The New Movement to Transform American Prosecution and End Mass Incarceration," (E. Bazelon).

The book that follows will be different. It will go through the looking glass to tell the story from the point of view of the defendant rather than the point of view of the lawyer. Most people are not lawyers and have no intention of ever becoming a lawyer. So that point of view is not intrinsically interesting to most people. But anybody could get arrested and most people are naturally fascinated with the topic. Could they handle it? Could they survive? Could they triumph? Some people just like to be prepared for worst case scenarios. This book will be for them a sort of jailhouse survivalist's manual.

Also, the accused's point of view is more heroic. He is one man alone, fighting for his life against the whole system. He is Samson fighting the Philistines in the Book of Judges. He is Howard Roark fighting the establishment in "The Fountainhead." He is Randall McMurphy fighting Nurse Ratched in "One Flew Over the Cuckoo's Nest." (N.B. two of those three lost.)

The stakes are never as high for the lawyer as for the accused. When a lawyer loses a case, he goes back to his house, pours himself a scotch on the rocks, and feels sad for an evening. When the accused loses, he gets sent to a jail cell to waits to be shipped to prison, often for the rest of his life.

Lawyers who write books have never been to prison. Sure, they've heard stories from their clients, but hearing stories about injustice and actually experiencing it first-hand are two different animals.

Lawyers who write books don't give advice to defendants about what they should actually do when they've been charged; or, rather, they give only one piece of advice to all defendants in all situations: hire a good lawyer.

This book will address and answer all the most important and most difficult questions that an accused person faces:

* How long will this all take?

* How can I find a good lawyer?

* How bad are public defenders?

* Can I trust my lawyer?

* Should I accept a plea offer and plead guilty?

* Should I go to trial?

* Can you give me any advice about jury selection?

* Should I take the stand and testify on my own behalf?

* How do appeals work? How long do they take?

This book will draw from an eclectic array of legal and literary sources:

* Supreme Court Decisions

* Criminal trial transcripts

* Constitution of the United States

* The Federalist Papers (James Madison and Alexander Hamilton)

* Leo Tolstoy, James Baldwin, Jonathan Swift

* The Gospel of John

* The Theory of Games (John Von Neumann and Oskar Morgenstern)

I truly hope this book will be useful to you or to your loved ones.

About Daniel Teitelbaum

Doctor Teitelbaum has a BS in Electrical Engineering, a BA in Painting, and a PhD in Engineering and Public Policy. He has served 28 months in county jail and over ten years in state prison. He has worked as a management consultant, a statistician, a legal clerk, a writing instructor, and a professional poker player. Dr. Teitelbaum is very much like a cup of yogurt that has exceeded its expiration date: most people would throw him away, but he is actually still quite tasty!

He has training in economics, psychology, statistics, risk analysis, and decision making under uncertainty. He has published one article in a peer-reviewed journal called Computational and Mathematical Organization Theory.

Dr. Teitelbaum would welcome your correspondence and can be reached by regular mail at the North Central Correctional Complex (NCCC):

> Daniel Teitelbaum A699663
> OPMC 884 Coitsville-Hubbard Rd,
> Youngstown, OH 44505

Through the GTL Getting Out app in the Google Play or Apple app stores;

Or email: CriminalJusticeThroughTheGlass@gmail.com.

Chapter 1: When You Get Arrested

When you get arrested, you will spend the night in the county jail. They'll take your clothes, your shoes, your wallet and any jewelry, and give you a jumpsuit and shower slippers and a mat to sleep on. In the morning, the jail's deputies will take you in handcuffs to court for your arraignment.[1] The arraignment is usually handled by a magistrate,[2] which is sort of like a junior varsity judge or a judge-in-training. If you have a paid lawyer, he will be there. If not, there will be a public defender there to represent you. The prosecutor will definitely be there and will read your charges aloud in court. The reading will include the names and numbers of the criminal codes and statutes (the law) that they say you violated.

After your charges are read, the magistrate will ask you how you plead. You will probably say, "not guilty." The magistrate will then set your bail and give you a trial date. Pay little or no attention to the trial date. You will not actually be going to trial on that date.[3] After your arraignment, you will be led out of the courtroom and put in a holding cell. Eventually, a deputy will lead you back to the jail cell where you spent the previous night.

If your charges were minor, then the magistrate will have given you a low bail or even an O. R. (O. R. = "Own Recognizance," = "you get to sleep in your own home that night without paying any money"). If your charges were a little more serious, you'll get a medium-sized bail, say,

---

[1] Arraign: v. 1. To bring before a court to answer an indictment. 2. To accuse or charge in general; criticize adversely; censure.
[2] Magistrate: n. 1. A civil officer charged with the administration of the law. 2. A minor judicial officer, as a justice of the peace or the judge of a police court, having jurisdiction to try minor criminal cases and conduct preliminary examinations of persons charged with serious crimes.
[3] See later chapters on "continuances" and "plea agreements."

between $5,000 and $50,000. Then you will be able to find a bail bondsman who will post your bail for a non-refundable fee of 10 percent. If, for example, your bail was set at $10,000, then you've got to get on the phone attached to the wall in your jail cell and call your dad, your girlfriend, your brother, your business partner – anybody – and get them to give $1,000 to the bail bondsman. You will probably swear up and down to them that you have the cash, and you will pay them back the minute you get out of jail and get to an ATM machine. Since you probably don't have $1,000 sitting around in a bank account, you will not actually be able to pay them back as promised. Congratulations! You've just lied to the most important person in your life. But don't feel too bad. Almost everybody in your situation would do exactly what you just did. It's hard to think clearly in county jail. Something about them dulls the mind. The lighting is bad. There's a lot of dust. They are crowded. They are noisy. You'll figure out how to scratch together $1,000 when you get out.

If the magistrate set a high bail, half a million or more, you would need to post at least $50,000 to the bail bondsman. That's $50,000 you'll never get back even if you are later found not guilty. Unless you are a doctor or a wealthy businessman you don't have that kind of cash lying around. Most drug dealers don't have close to that amount of money lying around. (Here is some free advice to drug dealers: dig a hole in the backyard of your mother's house. Put $5,000 in the hole. Cover it back up. Do not tell anybody about it. You will need it when you get arrested.)

Right now, you may be thinking, "$1,000,000 bail? No way! Doesn't the Constitution prohibit that?" Not really. The Eighth Amendment says, in part, "...excessive bail shall not be required, nor excessive fines imposed..." the key word here is "excessive." "Excessive" is a relative term; it is not absolute. That means that "excessive" means whatever the

3

hell the magistrate feels like it means. You might as well get used to this right now. Most of the things that you have been taught to believe protect you (e.g., the Bill of Rights) are just words. Words can be construed however the judge and prosecutor feel like construing them on that day. And neither of them cares what your opinion on the matter is. As such, all those protections are almost worthless to you, the defendant.

Lawyers and judges do not care about you. What they care about is money. So, when your bail is set, they are thinking less about "how high a bail is fair?" and more about, "how much money can this guy afford to pay?"

So, you're stuck sitting around in county jail.

You probably hate sitting around in county jail. Your lawyer, on the other hand, is thrilled about it. He will never admit this to you, of course, but he knows that every dollar you've saved for your entire life plus every dollar you can borrow from your parents and your grandparents is about to be chopped up and divided between the court and him. His eyes are lighting up with dollar signs. Secondarily - but also important - is that your lawyer wants as little to do with you as possible. When you are locked up, you can't drop by his office unexpectedly to make sure he is working hard and keeping all the promises he made to you. You can't call him on the phone - most law offices will not accept calls from jail cells. They say this is because all calls from jailhouse phones are monitored and recorded. That is true; they are. But the real reason they won't accept your call is because they are lazy. They know you're not going anywhere for months, and they don't want to deal with your frantic requests and suggestions. All of that is work. They hate work. And they especially hate unpaid work. They prefer that you speak only when spoken to. Eventually, when they have some free time, they will drop by the jail house and have one of the deputies go fetch you. When you're in jail, you're on call for them; they are not on call for you. Until your lawyer decides to see you, he doesn't want you bothering him.

If you are like most people, you probably believe that you are your lawyer's client and that a "client" is essentially the same thing as a customer, and "the customer is always right!" You probably believe that your lawyer is working for you, that he wants to do a good job by pleasing his clients and thereby develop a good track record and a good reputation which will lead him to get more clients in the future. The temptation to think this way is especially strong when you have already paid your lawyer a $10- or $15- or $25,000 retainer.

But once you are in a jail cell, none of that matters. You are no longer the customer. You are the product. Your lawyer, the prosecutors, and the judges all view you this way. To them, you are like a partially assembled product being conveyed down an assembly line, or like inventory stored on a warehouse shelf. They don't want to think about you at all until the time comes to ship you off to the next warehouse. Their job is to shepherd you down the conveyor belt from arrest to jail cell to plea bargain, and then to prison, with as little effort as possible.

In the case of the defense attorney, the math is pretty obvious: the less he works for each client, the more clients he can handle. The more clients he handles, the more money he gets paid. Volume, volume, volume.

They all work together on this. If this sounds unfair to you, that's because it is. The judge, the prosecutor, and the defense attorney all work together. They have been working together in the same building, the County Courthouse, for a long time, often many years. They may have gone to law school together. They might be members of the same country clubs. Their children may be friends or classmates. They know each other like coworkers at any company know each other. They don't know you. None of them are working for you. They don't like you, even though your lawyer pretends to. And even though you are supposed to be presumed innocent until proven guilty, they all presume you are guilty.

Now, where were we? Oh yeah, we were sitting in county jail just having returned from our arraignment. When you finally see your lawyer, he will pretend that you have a very strong case, the prosecution's case is full of holes, and you have a very good chance to win should you decide you want to go to trial. He is lying. It is an act. If your attorney is a lousy actor - and some are - and you are good at spotting insincere performances, fake smiles, and that kind of thing, then you may already be able to sense that he is lying.

Know this: lawyers never want to go to trial. Trials are very time consuming, and time is money to a lawyer. Trials involve pretrial motions and rulings on the motions and subpoenas of witnesses and jury selection and testimony by police officers and medical experts and then a sentencing. Lawyers and judges don't want that. What they want is all the money in your bank account followed by a nice plea agreement. That combination maximizes their profit and minimizes their effort expended, and that is how capitalism works. The prosecutor just wants a conviction, and all plea agreements will involve you pleading guilty to some of the crimes you've been charged with.[4] The judge does not want to go to trial either, mostly because he is old and lazy. All he wants is to clear his docket and get back on the golf course. He got his job by winning an election. He does not care at all

---

[4] Plea bargain: n. A process in which a defendant in a criminal case is allowed to plead guilty to a lesser charge rather than risk conviction of a graver crime.

about justice or your constitutionally guaranteed right to a trial by jury. Those things have no effect on his reelection prospects. He just wants you to admit that you're guilty and then shut up and go to prison. Everybody wants a plea bargain. The only person who doesn't know it is you, the defendant.

Your lawyer does not necessarily see what he is doing as dishonest, even though it obviously is. He believes - or pretends to believe - that by projecting confidence and acting as though he wants to go to trial, he will frighten the prosecutors into offering you a more generous plea.[5] Maybe this was true many, many years ago. I don't know. But nowadays it's a pathetic and obvious bluff. In the early stages, the prosecutor knows the strength of the case much better than the defense attorney does. The prosecutor has seen all the evidence and has pored through it multiple times while writing your indictment. Your lawyer probably hasn't looked at any of the evidence yet; and if he did, it was only to skim over a few of the most important documents that the prosecutor chose to show him. Also, the prosecutor knows that the defense attorney can't afford to take cases to trial. The whole business has devolved into an embarrassing pantomime designed to fool only you, the defendant.

1.1. Written Indictment

After your arraignment, the prosecution has 10 days to serve you your indictment in writing. If they fail to do this, you are released from jail. The jail is not allowed to keep you

---

[5] In many towns, you often see television commercials for law firms that say things like, "Want to get the best deal? Then hire a law firm that the insurance companies know is not afraid to take them to trial! Call the Law Offices of Palmer, Nicklaus, and Woods today!"

7

locked up longer than 10 days without a written indictment. Most likely, days will pass, and no indictment will be served upon you. Once you get to the eighth or ninth day, it is impossible not to get your hopes up that you won't be served. Impossible or not, you are hoping in vain. On the very last day, a deputy will get up from his desk, stroll over to the bars of your cell, yell your name, and present you with a folded piece of paper. That's your indictment.

Let's say you were riding in your friend's car. The cops pulled him over. You got out the passenger door and tried to run because there were drugs in the car, but they caught you and hauled you to jail. Your indictment might include something like this:

> F3 failure to comply (risk of harm) R. C. 2921. 331 (B)
>
> F5 possession of drugs R. C. 2925. 11 (a)
>
> M2 obstructing official business R. C. 2921. 31 (a)

"R.C." stands for "revised code." the number following the R. C. Is sort of like a call number for a book at a library. What you need to do is get a copy of your state's criminal law handbook and look up each code number. There you will find the precise definition of each crime you've been charged with. If you intend to take your case to trial, you need to know and understand each element of each crime. The prosecution needs to prove each element of each crime in order to secure a conviction.[6] At this stage, your lawyer is probably still pretending that he wants to go to trial. So, ask him which elements of each crime he expects the prosecution to have difficulty proving. If he replies,

---

[6] N.B. While this may be true in theory, it is not necessarily true in practice. See later chapters on trials and plea agreements.

"Remind me what exactly you were charged with again…?" then you can be pretty sure he doesn't want a trial.

Most county jails will not have a criminal law handbook for you to look at. Why would they? Nobody that works at the county jail, from the County Sheriff to the deputies, has any interest in improving your chances of going free. They're not going to spend money to provide inmates with useful legal materials unless it is mandated by law.

Every so often, one of the other inmates will have a criminal law handbook or some other useful reference and will be willing to let you borrow it. (He's probably not using it. A criminal law handbook is not the kind of book you read every night. It's the kind of book you look stuff up in every once in a while.) If not, see if you can get a family member to buy a used one and have it delivered to you at the jail. Alternatively, a family member could go to a local public library or a law library at a local university, look up the crimes by number, photocopy the relevant pages, and mail them to you in jail by regular US mail. Maybe by the time you read this it will be possible to find it all on the Internet.

If you are not planning to fight your case and you just want to take a plea as quickly as possible, then maybe it's not necessary to go to all the trouble of understanding the charges against you. Still, I think you should do everything in your power to research and understand your situation. I don't know why I think that. I just do.

I realize that there are many people in county jail who are illiterate or semi-literate who are not able to read difficult texts filled with legal jargon and convoluted instructions. I realize there are mentally ill, dyslexic, learning disabled, and brain damaged people who can't read a criminal law handbook. But there are also quite a few who could but don't because either they don't know it exists or because they're too lazy, apathetic, or defeated to fight back. That makes me sad. I don't know why. It just does.

1.2. Continuance

As the days and weeks go by in jail, you will notice that on most days, other inmates are being woken up early and brought to court. They are returned to the cell around noon looking dazed and sleepy. When you ask them, "What happened in court?" nine times out of ten, they will say, "Continuance."

As far as you are concerned, this means that something that was supposed to happen by a set date did not happen and had to be pushed back. Maybe the judge was supposed to rule on a motion to suppress an important piece of evidence but didn't: continuance. Maybe the prosecutors were supposed to turn over the transcripts of all of the police interviews. In fact, they say they did. But the defense lawyer says they did turn over the Smith interview but have so far not turned over the Jones or the Williamson interviews. The judge will say, "I've got a very busy schedule today! You sort this out between yourselves, and we'll meet again in three weeks. Continuance!" Or the defense was supposed to hire a mental health professional to come to the jail and determine the defendant's competence to stand trial and the defense lawyer says, "Well, we were trying, your honor, but first she was very difficult to reach, and now we finally reached her, but it's been hard to get her on the schedule at the jail…." Continuance!

Sometimes a continuance means they will actually push back the trial date; sometimes it doesn't. This is why it's hard to take any trial date seriously. Imagine that you were a high school student and you had a term paper due at the end of October. Imagine also that if the end of October arrives and you have not yet finished your term paper, you could simply say the magic word "continuance" and the due date would be pushed back to Thanksgiving with absolutely no penalty to you. How likely would you be to finish the term paper by the original deadline? Really?

1.3. Plea Negotiations

Each floor of the municipal courthouse has two large courtrooms, each presided over by a Common Pleas judge. Between the two courtrooms is a hallway with holding cells where defendants and prisoners sit while waiting for their hearings. The holding cells have stone floors, painted cinder block walls, two stainless steel benches jutting out of the walls, and a door made of vertical and horizontal steel bars. There is a stainless-steel toilet-plus-sink combo separated from the rest of the cell by a 4-foot-high cinder block partition. These cells (also called holding tanks) are usually extremely clean. The benches comfortably sit two people each. If there are more than four people in the cell, some sit on the floor, which, as I said, is clean.

You are usually brought to the holding cells around 7:30 AM. You will have all been up since before 5:30 AM, so you'll mostly just try to find a comfortable way to lean against a wall and close your eyes. The walls are cold, and the steel is cold, so it is hard to actually fall asleep, but not impossible.

At 7:30 AM, the judge usually has not yet arrived at his courtroom. His arrival time will depend on whatever time he has scheduled for his earliest court date for that day. Regardless, judges can arrive whenever they feel like it. They are the highest authorities in the building, so nobody tells them what to do.

Once the judge arrives, the prosecutors and defense attorneys can meet formally. Defendants never participate in these meetings; they just wait in the holding tanks. When the meetings are done, the defense attorneys walk out the side door of the courtroom into the hallway with the holding tanks. (Courtrooms usually have a back door that leads to the judge's chambers, and a front door for the public to enter and leave.) Then they find the cell containing their client, motion the client to the cell door and talk to him through the bars, bringing all the news about whatever he just finished discussing with the prosecutor.

Having sat in these holding cells for many days in a row, I was able to notice and learn things that most first-time defendants would miss.

Every day there is a stream of lawyers trudging back and forth between the courtroom and the holding tanks. They look like automatons play acting in a pre-scripted drama. It also may impress their clients; I don't know. Prosecutors make more money than defense attorneys, so they can afford to dress better. The public defenders are the worst. Their suits are not pressed. Their ties and shirts have slight stains on them that they hope you won't notice. Their leather shoes are scuffed. Younger lawyers sometimes do not know that they shouldn't wear a black belt with brown shoes.

One of the main reasons the defense lawyers go traipsing back and forth to the holding cells is to bring plea deals from the prosecutors to the defendants.

Almost all criminal cases end not with a trial but with a plea agreement. When I say, "almost all," I mean more than 95 percent of all cases. Trials may make the nightly news, but the criminal justice system runs on plea deals. So, understanding plea negotiations is far more important to most defendants than understanding trial.

By law, a defense attorney must present to his client any plea the prosecution offers. This law is almost completely unnecessary. The defense attorney wants his client to take a plea deal and get the case over with as badly as everybody else.

Here is an example of a discussion I heard between one defense attorney and his client concerning a plea offer:

The lawyer approached the cell door. His client, having waited all morning to hear the news his lawyer is bringing him, stands up and goes to the cell door without being called. The lawyer speaks just above a whisper, but all of us in the cell can hear every word. There is no privacy.

> Lawyer: "As we expected, the prosecutor has made you a plea offer. He's offering to dismiss both F5's, drop the F2 and F3, and you'll plead guilty to an F3 and F4."

(Let's call the defendant "D1")

> D1: "OK..."

> Lawyer: "They are going to recommend a sentence of three years for the F3, one year for the F4, served consecutively, for a total aggregated sentence of four years."

> D1: "What? Last time we talked, you told me no way I'd do more than a year and a half."

> Lawyer: "I know. But this is not an exact science. The offer is a little more than we expected; But it's still a pretty good offer and I think you should seriously consider it. Remember, you were looking at up to 12 1/2 years if they maxed you out on everything."

Defense lawyers are very practiced at delivering this particular piece of bad news. Like a funeral home director or an oncologist, they know how to look at you compassionately, remain respectfully silent while you vent your anger, and then gently but firmly guide you back to the business at hand. I doubt they teach this particular skill in law school, but any defense attorney who doesn't pick it up quickly won't last very long.

> D1: "No way. I can't do no four years. I can do two years, maybe, but even that's a stretch. I got a 2-year-old daughter. My baby momma ain't gonna be able to make it no four years. No way."

It's interesting that this guy has already relaxed his worst-case scenario from 18 months to two years. This is information that he should not reveal until the time is right.

> D1: "this ain't fair. When I came here this morning, I was looking at no more than a year, year-and-a-half. I told everyone in here I might get a year-and-a-half max but that I probably only have to do one. (He looks around and points expectantly at all of us sitting on the benches. We all dutifully nod our heads.)
>
> Lawyer: "I know."
>
> D1: "I don't know, man. Go back in there and tell them I'll do two years, but no more."
>
> Lawyer: "They are not going to offer two years."
>
> D1: "Well, did you tell them I got a baby and a job, and I'll lose my job?"

Lawyer: "I told them."

D1: "And did you tell them that this is my first offense other than a misdemeanor I got nine years ago?"

Lawyer: "Yes. I told them one hundred times. But they already know all this. They have access to your record."

This went on for several more minutes during which time the lawyers for the other defendants in the cell entered the hallway and began milling around behind his lawyer.

Lawyer: "Well, look. I'm holding up the line here. You think it over. I'll come back a little later."

The lawyer withdraws from the cell door and I can't see where he goes. The next lawyer - actually, it's two lawyers, if I recall correctly - comes to the cell door. Their client stands up from the bench. D1 sits back down in his place.

The conversation between the next defendant and his lawyers is uneventful and I don't recall what was said. When they are finished, their client sits back down seeming content and his two lawyers walk back to the courtroom. The hallway is left empty.

D1 stands back up, starts pacing around what little space there is, and immediately launches into a soliloquy.

D1: "This is complete bullshit. For months now he's been saying I was looking at one year. Once or maybe twice he said maybe, may-y-y-y-y-be they might try for a year and a half. But almost all we ever talked

15

about was one year. now, all of a fucking sudden he hits me with four? No way!"

The rest of us: "It's bullshit, man."

D1: "I can't do no four fucking years. No way. It ain't right."

The rest of us: "Well, tell him you won't plead to four years."

D1: "Four years? I told everybody I know I was gonna do one. I told my girl. I told my mom, my dad, my brother. I told the guys I work with. I told everybody."

The rest of us: "Well, tell him if they don't make you a better offer, you're taking that shit to the box."

That's how the cool kids say it. You can say "I'm going to trial" if you want to. But the cool kids say, "I'm taking that shit to the box."

This all continued for a while, him pacing around telling himself he'd rather stick his head in a garbage disposal than do four years in prison. [A brief philosophical aside: I've been in holding tanks where a guy who thought he'd be sentenced to 12 years ended up getting only nine and he was deliriously happy. Contrast that with D1 who just got offered four years and seems nearly suicidal. Clearly, the absolute length of the prison sentence is not what determines happiness or misery; it's the person's expectation and mindset that matters. Maybe that Buddha dude actually knew what he was talking about.] More griping by D1 ensued, replete with impassioned explanations of why four years was unfair: fatherly obligations, first offense, his crimes weren't all that bad when you really stopped to think about it, etc., etc. And he didn't think his lawyer was working hard enough to sell all this to the prosecutor. Then somebody had an original idea.

> The rest of us: "Tell your lawyer you want to talk to the prosecutor yourself."

> D1: "What?"

> The rest of us: "Dude, we believe you. You are way, way more convincing than your lawyer. If you tell your side of the story directly to the prosecutor, he might listen.

> D1: "I don't know."

> The rest of us: "All they can do is tell you 'no.' They're not gonna take the four years off the table just because you asked to talk to the prosecutor yourself."

> D1: "Yeah. Yeah. I don't know."

Like many defendants, D1 was phobic about talking to prosecutors and judges. It's an anxiety-filled experience combining a fear of public speaking with the dread that an elementary school student feels when sent to the principal's office. Twenty minutes or so later, D1's lawyer returned.

> Lawyer: "So, did you do any more thinking about the state's offer?"[7]

Many sarcastic answers leap to mind after a question like that. Here's one: "No, you asshole. I spent the last 30 minutes deciding whether or not I should buy a puppy."

---

[7] When you are charged in state court, the prosecution is usually called "the State." in federal court, it's called "the United States."

D1: "Yeah. You gotta get him to come down. Are you sure you can't get them to come down?"

Lawyer: "I'm sorry. Four is the best they're gonna do."

D1: "See if they'll do two. I'll do two years."

Lawyer: "They're not gonna do two. I've tried and tried. Four is the lowest they'll go."

D1: "Well, try again because four years is no good."

Lawyer (shaking his head): "I can't go in there and ask for two years. I'll just look like an idiot. They were quite clear they'll do four and no lower."

A long pause...

Lawyer: "If we take this to trial, you'll probably get more time. I mean, I'll fight like hell, but..."

Another long pause...

Lawyer: "Look, in about 10 minutes, I've got to go back into that courtroom and tell the prosecutor and the judge if you agree to their offer or not."

D1: "Well tell them I'll take two years."

Lawyer: "They are not going to agree to two years. I'm telling you. I've been through this a hundred times with them."

D1: "Well then tell them I want to talk to them myself. If I tell them myself, I think they'll listen to me."

Lawyer (shaking his head, looking at the floor): "It doesn't work that way."

D1: "Just tell them I want to come in there and talk to them myself."

Lawyer: "I can't do that. Look, I'll go in there and tell them what you said, but I guarantee they're not gonna budge from four years."

D1: "OK. But if they won't come down off for years then I want to come in there and talk to them face to face."

The lawyer walks away looking down, shaking his head. Twenty-five minutes later the lawyer comes back still looking down, still shaking his head. He approached the cell door. D1 hopped up and went to the door.

Lawyer: "Well, I don't believe it, but they are offering you two years."

D1: "They did? Really?"

Lawyer: "Yup. Surprised the hell out of me."

D1: "I fucking told ya!"

Lawyer: "Yeah, I know."

D1: "Four years was bullshit!"

Lawyer: "Yeah. Look, I'm guessing you want me to go back in there and tell them you'll accept their offer?"

D1: "Hell yeah, I'll accept their offer."

The lawyer nods his head and slinks away. He didn't seem very happy. When you think about it, he just got his client's sentence cut in half. So, if he cared at all about achieving the best outcome for his client, he ought to be happy. Instead, he slunk away like he just spelled a word wrong and was eliminated from a spelling bee. The rest of us were all high fiving and fist bumping in the holding cell.

End of story

Eventually, after you agree to the prosecution's offer, your lawyer will come back with a piece of paper for you to sign with the plea deal written on it (more on this later, but suffice for now to say that your plea deal journey is not over yet). Then, you are sometimes taken straight into court to plead guilty, out loud, on the record. Other times you are taken back to your jail cell and the actual pleading happens a week or two later. It just depends how busy everybody's schedule is, especially the judge.

The story you just read is instructive in several ways. First, it is very difficult and rare for defendants to get to see prosecutors or judges face to face. I presume this is because they intensely dislike spending time face to face with defendants and so have constructed the whole system in such a way that the distasteful bits are minimized and kept out of sight. You've probably heard the expression, "You don't want to see how the sausage is made." Well, the judge and the prosecutor don't want to see how the sausage is made even though they're the ones making the sausage. Explain that if you can....

The result is that the whole process resembles the childhood game of "telephone" where each plea offer goes from prosecutor to defense attorney to the defendant to the defense attorney to the prosecutor to the judge. Each link in the chain is an opportunity for wrong information to creep in and correct information to be lost.

Second, D1 woke up that morning expecting to be sentenced to one year in prison. He left that afternoon with an offer of two years in prison, and he is overjoyed. Just one of the many peculiar things that one sees in the bowels of the criminal justice system.

Third, the most important lesson here is that a defendant, in order to achieve the best outcome, often must overcome his own lawyer before he can overcome the prosecution. Most defendants expect to do battle with the prosecutors. They expect the judge to be a neutral and impartial arbiter. And they expect that the defense attorney is their ally in their fight against the prosecutor. But here we've just seen an example of a defense attorney fighting tooth and nail against his own client's best interest, trying to force him to accept four years in prison instead of two. Did the defense lawyer fight at all on his client's behalf during those closed-door negotiations with the prosecutor? There is no way for us to know. And I don't know that he didn't fight hard to protect his client's interest. All I'm saying is that we should not assume that he did. We should make our decision based on evidence. And what evidence do we have in this story that defense counsel was working for his client and not working for the prosecution? None.

Let's not be afraid to extrapolate from this example. Take the following hypothetical situation: before you were ever arrested, the police pounded on your door early one morning, showed you a warrant, searched your house, ripped a form off a clipboard that they were carrying, handed it to you and then marched back to their police van carrying your laptop computer, your cell phone, your files, cash that you had in your desk and a bunch of other valuable stuff. After getting over your initial shock, you notice a few things that seem amiss. The form they handed you a copy of had a box for your signature. But you never signed anything. So, it is blank. You call a lawyer if you didn't have one and you tell him all this. He says please fax him a copy of the form and he will look into it. So, you go to Office Depot and fax it to him and then you call him to make sure he received it, and he tells you again that he will look into it.

Do not trust him. He may "look into it," but he probably won't. I know that he just told you, twice, that he would look into it. But you should assume he is lying and call him and email him until he does what he promised.

If you are walking through the woods and you see a bear, you should not assume the bear is friendly. You should assume the bear is dangerous and take precautions. Similarly, I recommend not assuming that your lawyer will do what he promises. Assume he won't, and you'll live longer.

Chapter 2: Discovery

In order to get an indictment against you, the prosecution had to present its case to a grand jury. No defense attorney is present at a grand jury hearing and the proceedings are always secret. Because of this, it's impossible to know their winning percentage with certainty, but the prosecution is successful at getting an indictment just about 100 percent of the time. There is a famous saw that describes the fairness of grand juries, perhaps you've heard it: "they can indict a ham sandwich."

There is a sensible reason for keeping grand jury proceedings secret: privacy. It wouldn't be fair to those who are not indicted to have their reputations dragged through the mud. But secrecy invariably leads to corruption. And the fact that the original justification for the secrecy was reasonable doesn't provide any magical protection against corruption. So, how corrupt is it? When do they actually use corrupt means to win indictments that they couldn't get fairly? Believe it or not, I know the answer to that question. They use corrupt means whenever they need to.

Right now, I am imagining a prosecutor being interviewed on television saying, "Sure, there is a tiny amount of corruption. But the vast majority of prosecutors are virtuous, and the vast majority of indictments are obtained cleanly." If so, that is only because the vast majority of indictments don't require dirty tricks. Nobody cheats when they're going to win anyway. They only cheat when the outcome is uncertain, but cheat they do.

Baseball players cheat at baseball by taking steroids and by using high-tech surveillance equipment to steal signs. Cyclists cheat at cycling by taking steroids and hiding electric motors inside their bicycles. CEOs cheat at business by cooking the books. Wall Streeters cheat by insider trading. Students cheat on their college entrance exams. People cheat on their taxes. And all this cheating is being done with people watching. Nobody is watching the prosecutors. If you think they don't cheat, you are an idiot.

But I digress.

A key thing to realize is that when the indictment is issued, the defendant is not yet aware of it. There is as yet no defense attorney representing the defendant, but the prosecutor is in possession of all the evidence, and he has gone through it several times while preparing to present the case to the grand jury. What you as a defendant need to know is that the prosecutor has a huge head start over your lawyer. He was studying your case before you or your lawyer even knew it existed. This is why your lawyer's pretenses about how weak the prosecution's case is and how you will win at trial are so ridiculous.

Once you plead "not guilty" at the arraignment, the process of discovery begins, and the prosecution is required to turn over copies of the evidence to the defense. This can sometimes take a long time. There are police reports and medical reports that need to be photocopied. There are videos from security cameras and photographs of the crime scene that need to be copied to CDs. Lawyers are not computer people, so invariably half the videos and photos won't work when the defense attorney tries to open them on his computer. Weeks will go by before he figures out that a .JPEG is not exactly the same thing as a .GIF. Meanwhile, you sit in jail.

There are tape recordings of police interviews with witnesses, accomplices, and codefendants. Sometimes they need to be transcribed from audio to text. Sometimes they need to be redacted, i.e., have phone numbers, home addresses, email addresses, and Facebook home pages blocked out.

This may not be the end of the evidence, either. Just because you've been indicted and are sitting in jail does not mean they've stopped collecting evidence against you. One of the biggies is DNA evidence. When you were arrested, they probably took your fingerprints and a DNA sample. So now they're going to send your DNA sample along with samples they collected from the crime scene to see how closely they match. Sending stuff to a lab to be tested can take weeks or months. It doesn't happen overnight.

The prosecution doesn't have to turn over all the evidence to the defense, either. They get to decide what's important and what isn't. By law, they are required to turn over all evidence that is exculpatory. This was decided in the 1963 Supreme Court case Brady V. Maryland, where the court wrote, "the suppression of evidence favorable to an accused is itself sufficient to amount to a denial of due process." That sounds nice, but prosecutors and police routinely violate the law by not turning over evidence that might exonerate an accused or show that a witness for the prosecution is not trustworthy. And why shouldn't they? They never get punished for doing it. The worst that happens is maybe they are forced to turn over the evidence.

The mere fact that all the evidence goes to the prosecutor, and he then acts as a filter deciding what's inculpatory, what's exculpatory, what's useful, what's useless, and then picks and chooses what evidence to give to the defense, is unfair and conducive to corruption. The prosecution and the defense should both see all the evidence. Simple. But nobody in the system wants to do all that extra work. They all want you to take a plea.

Chapter 3: Bill of Particulars

After you receive your written indictment, make sure you ask your lawyer for your Bill of Particulars (BOP). The BOP is a statement of the factual details of your case, like where and when the crime took place, whom they say you robbed, what was taken, etc., etc. Your crimes will be described with far greater specificity in the BOP than in the indictment. Specificity always benefits the defendant. It is harder to prove specific charges than vague charges. For example, it is easier to prove that you stole some money than it is to prove that you broke into your neighbor's apartment and stole $486.74. Logically speaking, proving X is true and Y is true is more difficult than just proving X is true. For this reason, the prosecution may prefer not to give you the BOP. They may still have unanswered questions about the crime. They may even have aspects of the crime completely wrong. For example, they may say you committed the crime with Andrew and Chuck when in reality you committed the crime with Andrew and Brian, and you have no idea who this Chuck guy they're talking about even is.

So, the bill of particulars is a good thing. Get it.

Almost everybody is familiar with an indictment from watching cop shows on TV. But very few people who've never been arrested have even heard of a BOP. And most defense attorneys won't tell their clients about them. Many defendants never see their BOP and never know they should ask. Here's the thing: the defendant knows the particulars of what happened and what did not happen better than the defense attorney - usually because he was actually at the crime scene and the defense attorney was not. So, the defendant is generally more capable of identifying mistakes in the BOP than his attorney.

So, why are so many defense attorneys reluctant to get the BOP? First, they don't care much about it because they are not planning to take your case to trial. Second, defense attorneys dislike pestering or annoying the busy prosecutor by asking for the BOP. I'm not sure precisely what the deal is, but somehow the prosecutors have power over the careers of the defense attorneys they work with. As a result, defense attorneys do what they can to suck up. If the defense attorney angers the prosecutor, the prosecutor can punish him, his current clients, and his future clients by not offering plea bargains. Judges can punish defense lawyers by refusing to give court appointments that they need to keep their practices afloat.

As described earlier, your lawyer doesn't really work for you. He works for the court. The prosecutors and the judges also work for the court, but they are higher up in the organizational chart than the defense attorneys. So they are, for most intents and purposes, the defense attorneys' bosses. The upshot of all this is that the defense attorneys are more interested in kissing the asses of the prosecutors and judges than in helping their clients avoid jail time.

If you don't believe what I'm telling you, simply try this: don't mention the BOP to your lawyer at all. If he presents you with a BOP at any time before your trial, I will personally write you a letter apologizing.

Chapter 4: Your Rights in Practice

The bill of particulars (BOP) offers us an expedient starting point for understanding your rights in court and what they mean in practice. By law, you have a right to a BOP. The criminal rules of court in your state will say something like:

> "When the defendant makes a written request within 21 days after the arraignment but not later than seven days before trial, the prosecuting attorney shall furnish the defendant with a bill of particulars setting up specifically the nature of the offense charged and of the conduct of the defendant alleged to constitute the offence."

The word "shall" in the above paragraph is a command telling the prosecuting attorney what he must do. Anybody reading that can see that you get a BOP if you ask for one, right? Wrong. The missing element is this: what happens if the prosecuting attorney doesn't furnish the defendant with a BOP? Almost always the answer is nothing or almost nothing. When this is the case - which, as I said, is almost always - the right you are relying on disappears. Poof. Laws that are not enforced are not really laws at all. They are just suggestions. This only becomes apparent when you read the appeals of people who requested a BOP, didn't get it, appealed on those grounds, and lost their appeal. Time for an example:

> "Even if a bill of particulars was not provided, a defendant who has requested a bill of particulars waives error by proceeding to trial without receiving the bill or requesting a continuance."[8]

---

[8] Ohio v. Hickle (2004).

Here, the defendant requested a BOP, the prosecutor did not give it to him, and the trial happened anyway. The law commanded the prosecutor to provide it; but it turns out the prosecutor was not the one at fault, the defendant was at fault for *allowing* the trial to occur.

Here's more from the same ruling:

> "Moreover, appellant has not brought to our attention what additional useful information a bill of particulars would have afforded him."

What that last bit means is that even though you requested a BOP and the prosecution failed to provide it, you will not win on appeal unless you can tell the appellate court what information *would have been* contained in the bill of particulars *and* how that information would have helped you win your trial.

How on earth can you know what information *would have been* in a document that you never received? You can't. You can only guess. And even if you are able to guess, the appeals court can still deny your appeal simply by claiming that the missing information was not useful enough to merit a new trial. That's a little semantic trick that they pull quite often. They go from simply "is the information useful?" to "is the information useful *enough?*"

And that is how the law degenerates. You begin by reading a rule that says you have a right to a BOP if you ask for one; And you end up arguing whether the information that you imagine would have been included in the BOP that you requested, had it actually been provided to you, would have been useful enough to merit a new trial.

Right now, you might be asking, "That's why you need a good lawyer, right? You need someone who can win these arcane semantic arguments." I guess. The problem is that lawyers, especially defense lawyers, don't understand these legal fine points either. The proof is right there for you to see in the appellate court rulings that I quoted above. The appellate court judges wrote, "Appellant has not brought to our attention what additional useful information a BOP would have afforded him." That appeal was written by an appeals lawyer. The appeals lawyer clearly didn't know that he needed to bring to the attention of the appeals court any additional useful information that the BOP would have included. So, the appeals lawyer didn't know or understand the law. Anybody who did know and understand the law would at least have made an attempt to provide some. So, the appeals lawyer didn't know what he was doing. Q.E.D.[9]

Most lawyers who say they are good are bad. Some of them actually believe they are good. Most lawyers who actually believe they are good are bad also. So, how can you find a good one? I don't know.

"But they all passed the bar exam. So, they all have to be somewhat good, right?" I guess. I mean, I didn't actually see them pass the bar exam with my own two eyes. But I have seen with my own two eyes lawyers who stand in court and prattle like morons. And I have read with my own two eyes motions and appeals written by lawyers that were puerile and ineffectual. But everyone swears that they passed the bar exam. So, what can you do?

---

[9] Q.E.D. is an abbreviation of the Latin phrase *quod erat demonstrandum*, which translates to "which was to be demonstrated" or "that which was to be proved." In mathematics and logic, it's used at the end of a proof to indicate that the statement or proposition has been successfully proven. It essentially signals that the intended demonstration or argument has been completed.

Chapter 5: Trial Preparation:
Cutting Corners

The number and variety of crimes in America is vast. There is capital murder, aggravated murder, first-degree, second-degree, third-degree murder, and voluntary and involuntary manslaughter. There's burglary, aggravated burglary, robbery, theft, embezzlement, fraud, and receiving stolen property. There's rape, statutory rape, sexual assault, and gross sexual imposition. There's arson and kidnapping and a million kinds of drug crimes. The list is nearly endless. Each of these crimes has its own specific set of laws and rules of evidence that the lawyer is supposed to know. These laws and rules are interpreted and published mainly as "case" law. Case law is not constant. It changes over time.

Imagine for a moment a lawyer who is lazy, overworked, not especially good at his job, doesn't think his client has a chance in hell to win at trial and really just wanted his client to accept a plea the whole time anyway. Do you really believe that lawyer stays up late at night reading case law on the LEXIS - NEXIS database on his computer in order to make sure he's caught up on all the latest rulings that apply to his hundreds of clients? Doubtful.

Instead, what generally happens when the case goes to trial is this: the prosecutor does all the preparation and the defense attorney just copies off the prosecutor, similar to a lazy student who copies the homework of his more studious classmate. Defense attorneys do what they can to conceal this, but if you read the transcripts of enough trials, you will find plenty of instances where it is quite obvious.

The following is an example where first the prosecutor explains to jurors how they are required by law to weigh aggravating circumstances and mitigating factors together to decide whether they want to give a guilty defendant the death penalty; and then the defense attorney is given the chance to explain the exact same thing to the jury, but this time from the defense's perspective. The prosecutor is Ms. F. The defense attorney is Ms. M. This is taken from an actual capital-murder trial.

> Ms. F: Good morning. As the judge explained, I'm going to talk to you about the law in this case. We have to convince you of all the essential elements of the charges before you would find the defendant guilty of each of those charges. In that situation, you would then be called back for a much shorter proceeding for the sentencing phase to consider mitigation. And in the sentencing phase, the jury's responsibility is to weigh what the law calls the aggravating circumstances, which is the same thing as the specification.
>
> You're going to weigh that against evidence that's presented to you in mitigation. Mitigation tends to be things about the defendant: character, background, things about the defendant. And you then, as a juror, are required to consider anything that's presented in mitigation.
>
> You individually then decide whether it is of any weight to you. Do you find that to be a compelling piece of evidence? Do you not? And then you weigh them all together. Any mitigating evidence that you hear, you consider, and you decide how heavily to weigh it. And then you weigh that against the aggravating circumstance. These tend to be things about the crime. Mitigation tends to be things about the defendant. Once you've done that weighing, that's how you decide what the appropriate sentence is.

OK. I'd say that was fairly clear. Could have been tightened up a bit, but fairly clear. Now it's the defense attorney's turn.

Ms. M: Hello. My name is Ms. M. It is a lot to think about. And we talked about how many people don't really think about it until you're forced to. And a couple of you here are even saying different things than you said in your questionnaire, which is understandable. The jury together figures out, first of all, if there's even guilt. Right? There may not be. And if there is, then there's these other things as Ms. F. says, if the specifications are proved, right?

Then we get to weighing these factors against mitigation. That's done individually. Right? You are together as a jury. But there's no checkbox... there's no one—there's going to be instructions that the judge will give you specifically about how you do this. But that's an individual thing. And you - it sounds like you're kind of not sure either in terms of - I guess I want to hear you say that - could you follow the law that I was just talking about and Ms. F. talked about so well. Sometimes just hearing a different voice gets you to think about it a little differently. This is all if, if, if until you get down to here. And you each do this individually. You don't persuade each other. You respect each other's weight that you give to it. There is no pressure here. There is no - this is - could you follow that, do it. And if you were to come out this way, overweighing, could you consider that?

38

After reading these two excerpts, it's pretty easy to see who is going to win at trial, isn't it? Ms. F. is competent and prepared. Ms. M. is incompetent and unprepared. The key phrase to notice is where Ms. M says "... the law I was just talking about and Ms. F. talked about so well." The reason she says this is because she has not prepared herself one iota for this trial, she does not know the applicable law. She tried to learn it on the fly by listening to Ms. F. explain it to the jury. Then she stands in front of the jury and tries to restate in her own words what Ms. F. just said. She does a lousy job of it. (They never seem to show you this kind of lawyering on "Law and Order.") All Ms. M. needed to do was regurgitate the words she heard the prosecutor say, and she can't even do that.

Every aspect of the trial goes this way. The prosecutors prepare the case, and the defense attorneys try to coast through on the prosecutors' coattails. Sometimes even judges do it, too. Judges also want to do as little work as possible. Why not just let the prosecutors do all the research and just parrot their explanations? Judges usually have assistants and law clerks to help them do research, so the problem is not as pronounced. With defense attorneys, the problem is rampant.

Chapter 6: Hierarchy Of Needs in County Jail

The normal itinerary for a trip through the penal system looks like this: jail; correctional reception center; prison. Of the three, jail has the worst living conditions. This is somewhat counterintuitive because, generally, people in jail have not yet been tried or convicted and are supposed to be presumed innocent, whereas people in prison have been found guilty and sentenced.

Why are the guilty treated better than the innocent? There is no official answer to this question, or other policy document that mandates that jails be more unpleasant than prisons. But there are two guiding principles that cause things to be this way; the same two guiding principles that I have propounded in every other chapter of this book: lawyers and money. (Just add "guns" and we've got the makings of a Warren Zevon song.)

6.1. Lawyers

Every person you meet in county jail who has done time in prison agrees: prison is way better. They also agree that the reason it's like this is to get you to hurry up and take a plea. It works. Some people hate county jail so much that they take the first plea that the prosecution offers just so they can get the hell out of jail. Crappy living conditions in jails benefit both lawyers and judges by reducing the willingness of defendants to take their cases all the way to trial or to hold out for better plea offers.

6.2. Money

Prisons are run by the state. The money to run a prison comes from the state's budget. Jails are run by the county; their money comes from the county's budget. States have more money than counties. So prisons have amenities like softball fields, basketball courts, libraries, chapels, and educational facilities that jails don't have.

When you walk into the jail cell for the very first time, you will be wearing a short-sleeved vee-neck shirt made out of some industrial-strength cotton-polyester blend and a kind of pajama pants with an elastic waistband made out of the same material. You'll be wearing a pair of plastic slippers or flip-flops that you can wear right into the shower. These shoes will slip and slide all over the floor. This makes it harder for you to fight or make a run for it. Both of those activities require good traction. Lastly, you'll be wearing a plastic wristband with your inmate number laminated onto it.

You will be carrying a mat (about six and a half feet long), a blanket, a white sheet, a small white towel, a washcloth, a two-inch toothbrush, a two-inch-long tube of generic, industrial toothpaste, a motel-sized bar of soap, a plastic cup, and a roll of toilet paper. Find an open bunk and throw your stuff down on it. If all the bunks are occupied, find the least occupied corner of the floor that you can.

You might also have a little, pocket-sized bible. These rarely get confiscated when they search you. So write important names and phone numbers in the margins.

Jail cells contain metal bunkbeds, metal picnic tables with attached metal benches, a metal toilet with metal sink attached, a urinal, a shower, and a couple of telephones. That's it. You can see out easily and the guards can see in. The remaining walls will be made of stone or concrete. If you're lucky, there will be a window to the outside that lets in natural light.

Your first call using the jailcell phones can usually be made for free by typing in your inmate number, the number on your wristband. After the first one, you gotta pay. So the first call is usually made to a close relative asking them to please, please, please put a little money on your telephone account. They can accomplish this by calling some phone number and using their credit card or by going on the internet.

There will probably be a television that you can watch. It is usually situated outside the bars of the cell, beyond arm's reach. This makes it very hard to change channels, but inmates usually devise ingenious ways to get this done. There is usually only one TV for ten or fifteen inmates in a cell. This, of course, leads to fighting.

The only reason that jails allow inmates to watch television at all is so the jailhouse deputies can use the TV to control obstreperous inmates. Grown men charged with violent crimes will become quiet and compliant when a guard threatens to turn the TV off for 48 hours. It's embarrassing. Break your addiction to television! Rise above it!

If this is your first time in county jail, you have surely got a tremendous amount on your mind. There are so many things going wrong in your life all at once that it can be overwhelming. So I will categorize all these things for you and organize them into a kind of Maslow's Hierarchy of Jailhouse Needs: your first fight is against the prosecution. Your second fight is against the other inmates. Your third fight is against yourself. Your fourth fight is against friends and family on the outside. And your fifth fight is against boredom.

First, you need to try to get a lawyer who will actually do some work on your behalf. If you do nothing, the court will assign you a public pretender – that's what everyone calls public defenders. Some public defenders are OK; some are horrible; all are overworked. Some handle two or three hundred cases at the same time. This translates into roughly ten minutes per client per week. Contrary to public opinion, most paid lawyers are just as bad. It's hard to get them to do more than ten minutes' work on your case, either. They're also way more expensive. So pick your poison.

You need a lawyer who will bring you the bill of particulars and will bring you copies of all the discovery so that you can look through it and understand the evidence against you. You need to read the transcripts of all the police interviews of all the various witnesses and suspects. Your lawyer will have no way of discerning which witnesses are telling the truth and which are lying. You may need DNA experts, psychological evaluations, private detectives to track down witnesses, computer forensics experts, etc., etc. Your lawyer doesn't want to deal with any of this because once your money is spent, he intends to talk you into taking a plea bargain. So, if you want any of these things, you're going to have to fight hard against your own lawyer to get them. So that's your first fight in county jail: the fight to win your case.

Your second fight is against the other inmates in your jail cell. Here you will learn the following epigram: Hell is other people.[10] Every cell is different. Some are mellow; people just want to be left alone and they'll leave you alone. But some are a testosterone-fueled jungle with constant fights and oppression of weaker inmates. Inmates refer to these cells as "gladiator tanks." If you can defend yourself, you'll usually end up being left alone. If not, the other inmates will take everything they can from you, from your food to the stuffing in the mat that you sleep on. You can always call the guards and tap out. They will move you to a new cell or to a protective custody cell. There is tremendous shame in this. The inmates and even the guards will call you

---

[10] Jean-Paul Sartre, *No Exit* (1945).

a pussy and every other name they can think of. But if you gotta, you gotta. So that's your second fight in county jail: the fight against the other inmates in your cell.

Your third fight is against yourself. Maybe when the police arrested you, you were high on heroin or oxycontin. After a day or two in jail, you're starting to go into withdrawal: vomiting, headaches, diarrhea, you can't sleep; you moan a lot. Everybody wants you to just shut up so that they can sleep. It's sheer misery. But after three days, the worst of it is over. Maybe you're depressed. Maybe you're suicidal. Maybe you've been accused of some horrible crimes and you're deeply ashamed. Maybe you don't want your family to find out. Maybe you're afraid that you'll lose your job and you don't want your employer to find out. This is your third fight in county jail: the internal fight against yourself.

Your fourth fight is against your family, spouse, and close friends. When you're in jail, you need people on the outside to help you. This, in and of itself, is anathema to many men – men whose self-confidence and identity derives from their independence and ability to provide for others. Suddenly, they are reduced to impotence. But there are things on the outside that absolutely need to get done and you absolutely cannot do them from the inside. You might need a family member to look after your kids. You might need your girlfriend to feed your dog. You might need somebody to call your landlord, have the landlord let them into your apartment, grab the spare car keys from the kitchen drawer and move your car from the lot where it has been parked since your arrest before it gets towed. You may need help finding a lawyer. You may need people to put money on your telephone account or commissary account. You will see people in your cell screaming into the jailhouse telephones, "Bitch, after all the times I gave you money when you needed it, you can't come up with $25 to help me out?!?"

(Do not – I repeat – do not yell, "Bitch, I'm gonna beat the shit out of you when I get out of here if you don't…" These calls really are recorded, and that one sentence could turn into multiple felony charges including witness intimidation and aggravated menacing.)

These sorts of familial conflict can be extremely draining to the person in jail. There is a vast chasm between those on the inside and those on the outside. Those on the inside must expend huge amounts of time and energy to accomplish tasks that would be trivial on the outside. This is your fourth fight in county jail: your fight against family and friends.

Your fifth fight is against boredom. After you've gotten a lawyer and handled any legal exigencies, after you achieved safety and security from the other inmates in your cell, you've kicked your heroin habit, you've overcome your depression and decided that you want to continue living, you've severed communications with friends and family members who seem to prefer fighting with you to helping you, you shrunk your circle to just those people who give you aid, comfort, and strength, you can finally sit down on your bunk, take a deep breath, look all around you, and realize that there is nothing to fucking do. Boredom is now your arch enemy. If you can conquer it, you have conquered county jail. Jail will not be able to break you. You can last as long as it takes.

There is an invigorating satisfaction that comes from this. Like climbing a mountain, you have survived an ordeal. All your life, you have been told that this is rock bottom, that you must avoid this place at all costs. And now, here you are. It's bad, but you will live. You have taken the penal system's hardest punch, and you are still standing.

This can actually lead to profound happiness and contentment. Most inmates would not agree with that

47

statement. Most would say it's crazy talk. But most inmates lay around gloomily watching television or talking about what they're gonna do when they get out. But I have read descriptions of this happiness in classic literature several times. One of the best examples I have found is in "War and Peace," by Leo Tolstoy, where a character named Pierre gets taken prisoner:

> "...Pierre passed through hardships almost up to the extreme limits of privation that a man can endure. Owing to his vigorous health and constitution, of which he had hardly been aware until then; and still more owing to the fact that these privations came upon him so gradually that it was impossible to say when they began, he was able to support his position, not only with ease but with positive gladness. And it was just at this time that he attained that peace and contentment with himself, for which he had always striven in vain before...

> "...Pierre felt a new feeling of joy and vigor in life such as he had never experienced before.

> "And that feeling had not left him during the whole period of his imprisonment, but on the contrary had gone on growing in him as the hardships of his position increased."

Jail gives a man time to be alone, time to reflect, time to meditate. Many people take an inventory of all their desires and all the goals they were so doggedly pursuing before jail. They realize that most are superficial and trivial and would not bring much real happiness if accomplished. They jettison those desires and they become happier. As I say: most people in jail do not achieve this insight. But some

48

do. I encourage you to try; Or, if not to try, at least to be open to it, should it find you.

Chapter 7: Finding a Good Lawyer

Let's say that you're a guy with a couple thousand dollars in the bank and a good job with a salary of $85,000 per year. One night, a guy in a bar starts a fight with you. You break his jaw. The cops show up. They arrest you, not him. You spend the night in county jail. You are arraigned the following morning where you find out that you are being charged with felonious assault, a second-degree felony with a maximum penalty of eight years in prison. The magistrate sets your bail at $20,000. You find a bail bondsman, pay $2,000, and bond out.

You decide you want a paid lawyer. You've heard nothing but nightmarish descriptions of public pretenders. But you don't know any lawyers. So, how do you find a good one? You talk to your mother and to a guy at work who is a pretty good friend. The guy at work doesn't know any lawyers and asks, "why don't you just look in the Yellow Pages?" Your mother has an old friend who is a lawyer and says she will ask him. This friend, it turns out, is a corporate lawyer. He says he doesn't know any criminal defense lawyers, but he promises he'll ask around for you. A few days later, he sends you a text message: "a defense lawyer named Joshua Miller has a very good reputation. Phone number 555-4321." You call the number. The secretary puts you through to Mr. Miller. You describe what happened that night in the bar, pointing out that the other guy hit you first. Mr. Miller wants a $2,500 retainer to take your case.

Now, here is what you need to know. I quote the author James Baldwin:

> "But I was to discover that to have a "good" reputation as a criminal lawyer does not necessarily reflect any credit on said lawyer's competence or dedication; still less does it indicate that he has any interest in his clients:

52

the term seems to refer almost exclusively to the lawyer's ability to wheel and deal and to his influence with other lawyers and judges, and district attorneys. A criminal lawyer's reputation—except, of course, for one or two titans in the field—would appear to depend on his standing in this club. The fate of his clients depends, to put it brutally, on the client's money: one may say generally that, if a poor man in trouble with the law receives justice, one can suppose heavenly intervention."[11]

Those words were written in the late 1960s, and they are at least as true today as they were then. The American criminal justice system has not gotten any fairer since the 1960s, and may have grown less fair. Do you know of any major legislation designed to protect the rights of the accused or crack down on crooked lawyers that has become law in the last 50 years? Of course not. Can you recall a single press conference by a congressman or senator decrying the unfairness of his state's courts and demanding stricter supervision of criminal lawyers? Of course not. Do you recall any major legislation designed to take rights away from accused criminals in order to allow courts to be tougher on crime? Yep. There was the Racketeering and Interstate Criminal Organizations (RICO) act written to fight the mafia and other criminal syndicates. There was also an omnibus crime bill passed during the Clinton administration. How about legislation designed to take away the rights of accused in the name of protecting America against Islamic terrorism? Sure. There was the anti-extremist terrorism and death penalty act (AETDPA), which eviscerated the right of habeas

---

[11] James Baldwin, *No Name in the Street* (1972).

corpus.[12] There was also the "PATRIOT Act" passed during the Bush II administration. By and large, the American people seem to love all this. The more the constitutional rights of accused criminals are rescinded, the happier they get, presumably because it makes them feel safer.

Either way, you're caught in the trap now. You have no idea which lawyers are good, and which are bad. Maybe they are all bad. This Miller guy you spoke to says you have a strong case and he'd be happy to take your case to trial. Don't believe him. He just wants that $2,500 retainer fee. He has bills to pay. As soon as your check clears he will bring up the possibility of a plea bargain. You can call around. You can talk to other criminal lawyers. They will all put on a brave face for you. What you really ought to do is talk to each lawyer's former clients. See how they feel. Were they happy with the defense they received? But how do you go about finding them? Most of them are in prison. Regardless, you emptied your bank account to pay the bail bondsman and get you out of jail. You can't afford the priciest lawyers. There are no easy answers for you.

Some of the lawyers you talked to will tell you things like, "your case will probably be assigned to judge Cochran's courtroom. I play golf with Judge Cochran every month," or "my wife and judge Cochran's daughter are best friends. They went to high school together." You should be very skeptical and wary of these sorts of claims.

In essence, they are part of a confidence game, and you are being conned. You're in a very vulnerable position, having been charged with a serious crime that you do not believe was your fault, and are, therefore, unusually credulous. You understood that the lawyer was insinuating

---

[12] More on habeas corpus in a later chapter.

that his good relationship with the judge will get you a more favorable outcome and you very much want to believe it. Don't. That lawyer's insinuation has an obverse that you are not seeing: if the lawyer is buddies with the judge, then the judge is buddies with the lawyer. Judges don't do favors for defense lawyers; defense lawyers do favors for judges. Like, when your lawyer plays golf with that judge, the judge will tell him that he has a very crowded docket, and he would very much appreciate it if he could get you to hurry up and plead guilty. Your lawyer will then promise the judge that he'll do his best to convince you because he is hoping to gain favor in the judge's eyes.

That is the way the criminal justice system actually works. It makes no difference to your lawyer whether you win or lose your case. He makes the same amount of money either way. If you win your case, he's happy. If you lose your case, you go to prison, and he'll never see you again. But winning the judges favor? That may benefit him in the future. So that is what will happen. And in a way, you deserve it. You got greedy. You thought that lawyer was going to get you special treatment that you didn't really deserve. And that is how con games work.

Chapter 8: Can You Tell Your Lawyer the Truth?

During your long journey from arraignment to trial, there may come a point where your lawyer asks you, "So, did you do it? It's okay to tell me. It won't affect the way I defend you, and everything you say to me is privileged and confidential." This question is typically asked in a private meeting room where just you and your lawyer are present.

How should you answer? You may be completely guilty. You may be mostly guilty but not guilty of everything you've been charged with. You may be just a little bit guilty. Or you may be completely innocent. It all makes no difference. Your answer to your lawyer must be, "I am one hundred percent completely innocent."

Every state in the USA has a "Professional Code of Conduct" to which lawyers are supposed to adhere. In that code will be something like the following:

Rule 612: It is professional misconduct for a lawyer to do any of the following:

> (a) Violate or attempt to violate the State Rules of Professional Conduct, knowingly assist or induce another to do so, or do so through the acts of another.
> (b) Engage in conduct involving dishonesty, fraud, deceit, or misrepresentation.

Based upon that code, if you ever tell your lawyer that you are anything less than one hundred percent innocent, your lawyer will never say to the prosecutor or the judge that you are innocent, or to the jury, should you end up going to trial. The most he will say is that the evidence is not strong enough to convict you – and even that will be said half-heartedly, almost apologetically. When that happens, you cannot win.

If you confront your lawyer during a private meeting and pound your fists on the table and demand that he tell the jury that you are innocent, he will reply, "I can't do that. I might lose my job." Meanwhile, prosecutors and police routinely lie, exaggerate, and misrepresent the evidence against you with complete impunity. Have you ever heard of a prosecutor being fired for lying or a policeman being reprimanded for lying? Lying should be part of the police motto: "To protect, serve, and lie under oath."[13]

Your lawyer's belief that you, his client, are guilty, will sometimes manifest during his examination of witnesses. For example, he may be examining a witness who believes that you are innocent. You may notice that your lawyer grills this witness a little harder than he did all the witnesses who said that you were guilty, probing for inconsistencies in their testimony, asking tough questions multiple times, and conveying with his body language and tone of voice that he doesn't believe the witness' testimony. And you will wonder, "Why is he doing this? He's acting like a second prosecutor, not like someone I am paying to defend me."

Incidentally, your lawyer's claims that everything you tell him is privileged and confidential are dubious. Your lawyer and the prosecutor have been working together for a long time. They can communicate with facial expressions, sideways glances, and clever phrasings. And I remind you that your lawyer is far more interested in sucking up to the prosecutor than in fighting for your freedom.

Here is something you can try for fun: plant false info during a private meeting with your lawyer. Tell him in confidence that you hid money or the murder weapon in the garage of an old friend of yours. If the prosecution suddenly comes up with a search warrant for that garage, you will

---

[13] Line stolen from a George Carlin comedy special on HBO.

know with certainty that your lawyer is passing your "privileged" information to the prosecutor.

Chapter 9: The Underground Economy

In every jail cell and every prison yard,[14] there are people with money who want work done and people without money who are willing to work. These two things are all that is needed to create an underground economy: supply and demand.

The Bible says, "for the wages of sin is death..." (Romans 6:23). But after spending a day or two in jail, you learn that the wages of sin are ramen noodle soups, Little Debbie snack cakes, packets of Hi-C Kool-Aid, bags of Cool Ranch Doritos, and stamped envelopes. These are bought from a store, usually called a "commissary" or a "canteen." Every prison has one. Inmates can buy snack foods, hygiene products, medicine, stationery, playing cards, etc. The meals in county jail are small. Inmates are constantly hungry and bored. So snacking is a big part of daily life. Stores also sell medicine. Life without ibuprofen or athlete's foot powder or hemorrhoid cream can be miserable. It's impossible to maintain a tolerable existence without occasionally buying stuff from the store.

Some inmates get all the money they need sent in by family members on the outside. They can get whatever they need from the store whenever they need it. Those who don't have money coming in have to hustle for it. This is commonly referred to as "living off the land."

In prison, the main hustles are: doing people's dishes, doing laundry, sewing and tailoring people's clothes, artwork (there is a surprisingly robust market for portraits, greeting cards and hand-decorated envelopes), letter writing and legal writing, tattooing, and carpentry and electronic repair. You can also make quite a bit of money running a sportsbook, loan sharking, or brewing hooch (hooch is

_____

[14] I will use 'jail' and 'prison' interchangeably in this chapter.

alcohol made by fermenting orange juice, canned fruit, or ketchup). These last three are quite lucrative but the people who do them usually end up getting caught and have to do some time in the hole ("the hole" = solitary confinement).

Of course, the big, big moneymaker in prison is dealing drugs. Drugs must be smuggled in. This drives the prices up—way, way up. On the street, 1/4 ounce of marijuana costs $50, typically purchased in a plastic baggie. Inside the prison walls, marijuana is sold in the little white cap of a stick of Chapstick. One Chapstick capful of marijuana sells for $50. So, if 1/4 ounce equals 30 Chapstick caps, then 1/4 ounce is worth about $1,500 on the inside.

There is a similar market for tobacco. One cigarette from a pack of Marlboros, once inside the prison, gets broken down into four or five thinner, hand- rolled cigarettes. Each of these then sells on the prison yard for four or five dollars. So each cigarette winds up selling for about $20. Each cigarette. There are twenty cigarettes in a pack, so a $10 investment produces $320-$500 in revenue.

Harder drugs are available, too: pills, strips of suboxone, whatever can be smuggled easily. Drugs enter the prison in five ways.

> 1) Through the mail. A piece of writing paper can be soaked in LSD and then mailed in an envelope along with a regular letter. If the people working security at the prison mailroom don't notice, that sheet of paper can be cut up into tabs of LSD and sold for who-knows-how-much on the yard.

> 2) Packages thrown over the fence. Most prisons are located in rural areas. The fences that encircle the prison are about ten feet high and have razor wire on top. So, a guy on the outside hides in the cornfields or in the woods near the prison fence. He runs up

with a package full of drugs and he heaves it over the fence when nobody is looking. Then, his partner on the inside runs up to the fence and picks up the package, also when nobody is looking. If they can pull this off, it translates into thousands of dollars in profit.

3) Visitation. Prisons allow inmates to have face-to-face visits with family and friends. A small amount of hugging and kissing is permitted as well as sitting together eating food purchased from vending machines. Prisoners are strip-searched before and after visits. But the guards doing the searches are lazy, careless, and poorly paid. So drugs slip through, usually in small quantities.

4) Volunteers. Prisons have outsiders come in to lead religious programs, teach courses, run job fairs, and other such things. They sometimes get co-opted or tricked into bringing contraband into the prison.

5) Corrections officers and full-time staff. These people enter and leave the prison every day. They just smuggle the drugs in when they come to work and then hand them to an inmate partner. The inmate takes the drugs and sells them on the yard. That inmate's friend or family member on the outside then pays the corrections officer (C.O.) in cash for his share of the profit. For the C.O., all money changes hands outside the prison. His only job is to bring the drugs in without getting caught and hand them to his confederate.

This is far and away the most common way for drugs to enter the prison. For a C.O., the economics are too attractive to resist. A simple handoff of a smuggled package to an inmate might be worth $750, tax free. Corrections officers get paid about $15 per hour. That's about $600 per week before taxes. Unless they live with their parents, they can't survive on that. So they smuggle drugs into the prison and double their salary until they get caught. When they get caught, they just get fired. They can go get a new job at Wendy's or Home Depot. Getting fired from a low-paying job that you hate is really more of a reward than a punishment, when you think about it.

So, drugs are always available on the prison yard. The prison administrators are always inventing new rules and regulations designed to eliminate them. But so far, they've always failed.

Chapter 10: Time

Lawyers and judges can warp time in ways that would make Albert Einstein feel seasick. I'll give you 3 examples: juvenile offenders, felony sentencing, and speedy trial rights.

10.1. Juvenile offenders

You've probably heard that the law treats juveniles more leniently than adults. This makes sense because juveniles are less responsible than adults. Their brains have not finished developing. They are not allowed to drive a car. They can't vote. They can't buy alcohol. But as with all laws, there are exceptions; and the exceptions let the courts try juveniles "as an adult" whenever they feel like it. Obviously, if they can try a juvenile "as an adult" whenever they feel like it, then being a juvenile is no protection whatsoever.

More generally, rules can be entirely invalidated by their exceptions. If I were to promise my wife that I would be faithful to her always and completely, except for "whenever-the-hell I feel like cheating on her," that wouldn't be a promise at all. In the criminal justice system, worthless promises of this sort are commonplace.

Let's take a closer look at some of the exceptions applied to two juveniles because they are truly mind-bending.

In Ohio, they have a law, O.R.C. 2152.02 (C) (3) that allows 14-year-olds to be tried as adults:

> Any person who, while under 18 years of age, commits an act that would be a felony if committed by an adult and who is not taken into custody or apprehended for that act until after the person attains 21 years of age is not a child in relation to that act.

You read that right. Ohio circumvents its own law by somehow saying that your age when you committed the crime is not important. What's important is the age at which you were taken into custody. It's nonsense. The whole reason juveniles were treated leniently in the first place is because their brains were less developed at the time they committed the crime. The development of their brain when they are apprehended is entirely irrelevant – or, it should be, anyway.

Also, a close reading of O.R.C. 2152. 02 (C) (3) suggests to me that the accused is being presumed guilty, not innocent. It says if a juvenile commits an act... then that person gets tried as an adult. But the trial is supposed to determine whether or not the accused committed the act. So, in order to try them as an adult, you have to presume them guilty before you try them, no?

These exceptions can have catastrophic consequences for the accused. If you commit a crime when you were 17 - or are simply accused of a crime - the police can decide to wait until you are 18 (or 21) and then arrest you, so now you're facing serious, serious time. If a high school student gets accused of having sex with a girl at a party who could not properly give consent because she was drunk, the police could simply wait until the boy turns 18. now when they arrest him, he's facing a possible life sentence. He'll definitely plead guilty rather than face life in prison.

In Oklahoma, they sentence a 15-year-old to death[15] using a statute that allows juveniles to be tried as adults when (1) the prosecutor shows the prosecutive merit of the case; and (2) the court finds there are no reasonable prospects for the rehabilitation of the child. Notice the keywords "merit"

---

[15] Thompson v. Oklahoma (1988).

and "reasonable" rearing their ugly heads. They mean that the court can try a child as an adult whenever they feel like it.

Wouldn't it be nice if you and I could apply these same exceptions whenever we wanted to? Imagine a 16-year-old boy buying a case of beer from a liquor store.

> *Clerk: you can't buy alcohol. You're a minor.*
>
> *Boy: I know that; But I'm buying this beer "as an adult."*
>
> *Clerk: well, OK then. Here you go.*

Exceptions weaken laws. That's obvious. What's less obvious is that weakening laws strengthens lawyers. If the law says that a person under the age of 18 who is accused of a crime MUST be tried as a juvenile, then lawyers have no power to circumvent the law. But as soon as the law has exceptions that contain vague words like "reasonable" or "merit," suddenly it's up to some lawyer somewhere to decide whether the accused is tried as an adult or as a juvenile, which is a tremendous amount of power to wield over someone's life.

The laws in your state were written by the legislature. State legislatures are comprised almost entirely of lawyers. Then those laws are put into effect in courts where they are interpreted by whom? More lawyers. Lawyers tend to interpret laws in ways that benefit lawyers. Over time, the laws become weaker and weaker while lawyers become stronger and stronger. It does not require a belief in some sinister conspiracy to understand this. Lawyers, like all people, behave in ways that benefit themselves. Left unchecked, the system will inevitably reach the state it is in now: the law does not control the lawyers; The lawyers control the law.

10.2. Felony Sentencing

Class	Minimum Sentence	Maximum Sentence
F1	3 years	11 years
F2	2 years	8 years
F3	1 year	5 years
F4	0.5 years	1.5 years
F5	0.5 years	1 year

There are five classes of felony, listed as F1 through F5. Each carries a minimum allowable sentence and a maximum possible sentence. Within those ranges, the judge gets to decide.

Example 1: let's say you were found guilty of an F1, an F3, and an F5. The judge sentenced you to four-and-a-half years on the F1, two years on the F3, and six months on the F5 for an aggregate sentence of seven years. You appeal your conviction. The appellate court vacates your F3 and your F5 but upholds your conviction on the F1. They remand your case to the trial court to receive a new sentence on the F1 only. This time, the judge (the same judge who sentenced you the first time) decides to give you 9 years on the F1 because he didn't like that you had the temerity and bad manners to appeal your conviction. Voilà! You are now guilty of two fewer crimes, but your sentence just grew by two years.

Example 2: let's say you were found guilty of four F3s and the judge sentence you to five years on each one. sounds like a 20-year sentence, right? Rarely. Most people outside of the criminal justice system are not aware of this, but combinations and permutations are also possible. You could be sentenced to serve three of them concurrently and the fourth consecutively. That would take 10 years to complete.

10.3. *Speedy trial*

In theory, if you are out on bond, the state has 270 days to bring you to trial on felony charges. If you are in jail, not out on bond, each day counts as three days (yet another example of time-bending), so the state has 90 days to bring you to trial. But as with all laws, there are exceptions, and the exceptions are more important than the law.[16]

One such exception is that the state will be granted an extension of time for any "delay occasioned by the neglect or improper act of the accused." In practice, this means they can get a time extension whenever they feel like it and they can blame it on the accused.

---

[16] As Tom Waits said, "the large print giveth; and the small print taketh away."

Chapter 11: Pretrial Motions

A few weeks before your trial is scheduled to begin, your lawyer will file a bunch of pretrial motions. These motions will be perfunctory and of little consequence: a motion for your right to wear civilian clothes to trial instead of your jail uniform, a request that all sidebar conversations between judge and lawyers be recorded, etc. The fact that your lawyer filed these motions does not mean that he is actually preparing to go to trial. He still intends to talk you into accepting a plea offer, but you're close enough to trial now that he has to file these motions, just in case.

Lawyers love these pretrial motions when they have a paying client. The motions are pure boilerplate. Your lawyer will just grab a copy of one that he or a colleague wrote before somebody else's trial. Then he will replace the previous defendant's name and case number with your name and case number and submit it to the court. It takes about 10 minutes in Microsoft Word to do this. But he can bill for it as if he stayed up all night writing it himself and sweated over every word.

Sometimes, they even screw up the copying and pasting and you can find the names and/or case numbers of their former clients in various spots in "your" motions.

Chapter 12: Receiving Stolen Property

In my state, there is a law against receiving stolen property. It reads, "no person shall receive, retain, or dispose of property of another knowing or having reasonable cause to believe that the property has been obtained through commission of a theft offence."

Here's a brain teaser for you: how can a criminal defense attorney represent a bank robber, a mugger, a cat burglar, or a stickup artist?

When a mugger gets arrested, he hires a lawyer to defend him. The lawyer requires a $1,500 retainer in order to take the case. So the mugger pays him - in cash. Where does the lawyer think that money came from? It came from the little old ladies that the mugger mugged, obviously. And those little old ladies would like to get their money back. But they're not going to get it. The lawyer gets it.

Robbers and muggers don't have high-paying side jobs as dental hygienists or certified public accountants. Their money comes from their crimes. So how can a defense attorney accept $1,500 in cash from his brand-new mugger client? Brand new "alleged" mugger client - excuse me. He is clearly receiving stolen property.

If you think about it, nearly all the money that criminal defense lawyers make is dirty money. When you watch the trial of Bernie Madoff, he is sitting next to two or three $500-per-hour defense attorneys. When you watch the trials of John Gotti or Pablo Escobar or Saddam Hussein, they are seated next to two or three $500-per-hour defense lawyers. All of that money that those defense attorneys are putting into their pockets was at some earlier time in the pockets of people who earned it by working. Those working people gave their money to Bernie Madoff to invest for them in the stock market. Those working people gave their money to Escobar's legions of drug dealers so that they could get high. But in the end, it all wound up in the pockets of lawyers.

All of this wonderful commerce is made possible by the word "reasonable" in the criminal statute that prohibits receiving stolen property. Lawyers simply argue that they did not have "reasonable cause to believe" that the property had been "obtained through commission of a theft offence." This is ridiculous, of course. But district attorneys have the power to decide which crimes get charged and which do not. District attorneys are lawyers. They went to law school. So they make decisions that benefit lawyers and do not make decisions that hurt lawyers. They know that if criminal defense lawyers were not allowed to receive stolen money, that would be the end of a very lucrative income stream for lawyers as a group. The more money that flows into the pockets of lawyers - any lawyers - the better it is for the legal profession as a whole. These lawyers can then use this dirty money to repay the student loans they took to go to law school. This in turn allows law schools to keep their tuitions sky-high. All the lawyers benefit.

All the law professors teaching at all the law schools in this country know this. Whether any particular law professor has thought deeply about the way that money flows through his particular corner of the legal economy, I can't say. But at some level - consciously or unconsciously, implicitly, tacitly - they know where their money comes from.

So when some second-year law student raises his hand and asks his professor whether it is moral that Saddam Hussein's lawyers are spending the money that Saddam stole from the people he murdered with poison gas, that law professor will rub his chin contemplatively and give a well-rehearsed answer about the costs and benefits to society of fair trials for all accused people, no matter how heinous their crimes, followed by the preordained conclusion that the marginal benefits outweigh the social costs and that, yes, it is moral for lawyers to take that money, baby.

Chapter 13: Reasonable Doubt

The concept of "reasonable doubt" is a cornerstone of the American criminal justice system. But what does it really mean? Nobody knows. Nobody can define it. Even the U.S. Supreme Court has admitted as much: "The government must prove beyond a reasonable doubt every element of a charged offense. Although this standard is an ancient and honored aspect of our criminal justice system it defies easy explication."[17]

At the end of every trial, the jury is given written instructions and then sent back to a room to deliberate (appropriate word, DE- liberate) until they reach a verdict. Those written instructions will include an attempt to define "reasonable doubt." These definitions are always worse than useless; they are confusing and obscure. For example, here is the definition given in the California Penal Code:

> "Reasonable doubt is defined as follows: it is not mere possible doubt, because everything relating to human affairs is open to some possible or imaginary doubt. It is the state of the case which, after the entire comparison and consideration of all the evidence, leaves the minds of the jurors in that condition that they cannot say they feel an abiding conviction of the truth of the charge."

I think you will agree that definition is terrible. You probably understood what reasonable doubt was better before you read the definition. The gist of the definition is: reasonable doubt = you lack an abiding conviction of the truth.

---

[17] Victor v. Nebraska (1994).

What does that mean, anyway? Quick, off the top of your head, what does the word "abiding" mean?[18] And the word "conviction" just means you are convinced beyond a reasonable doubt. The whole definition is nothing more than saying, "beyond a reasonable doubt means that you don't have any doubts that are reasonable." It is circular and useless.

And what does "imaginary doubt" mean? All doubts are imaginary. That's where doubt takes place: in the imagination of the doubter. Is it really true that "everything relating to human affairs is open to some possible or imaginary doubt?" I have no doubt whatsoever that the Tampa Bay Buccaneers beat the Kansas City Chiefs in Super Bowl LV. I am 100 percent certain. I have no doubt; Imaginary or otherwise. So, no, it is not true that everything relating to human affairs is open to doubt.

So, they can't define reasonable doubt. What's the big deal?

First, they pretend that they do define it. They should just admit the truth: they can't. But that would make them look bad. So they create these obscurantist definitions to make themselves feel good, not to actually help the jurors reach a proper verdict. It is dishonest of them to pretend when they know they can't define it. The US criminal justice system is filled with hundreds and hundreds of these little lies. What do we call someone who tells hundreds and hundreds of lies? A liar. Lawyers and judges, as agents of the criminal justice system, are forced to repeat these lies so often that they must end up believing them.

Second, in an ideal world where defense attorneys were actually fighting back against prosecutors, the problem

---

[18] Abiding: adj. Continuing without change, enduring, steadfast.

might not be so bad. But in the real world where prosecutors do all the work and defense attorneys just nod their heads submissively, most jurors go into deliberations believing that "beyond a reasonable doubt" is the same thing as "pretty sure." So nowadays, that's all it takes to get a conviction: pretty sure.

Chapter 14: Should You Plead Guilty or Go to Trial?

This is the single most important decision that you as a defendant have to make. So we'll spend a fair bit of time on it.

If you've been reading this book expecting to find some magical advice that's going to get you out of the trouble you're in, then for you, this book is sort of like the play "Waiting for Godot," by Samuel Beckett. Spoiler alert: Godot never shows up. Sorry to disappoint you. And now I have to disappoint you again: you should almost certainly take the deal and plead guilty, whether you committed the crime you are accused of or not. Hold out as long as you can. Get the best offer you can. And while it pains me very much to have to say this, it all boils down to a math problem, and the answer is very clear: take the deal and plead guilty.

The best way to understand this is by looking at a real-life example:

You are facing a maximum sentence of 12 years for a variety of felonies. The prosecution offers to let you plead guilty to one F3 - they will drop all the other charges - and say that they will recommend that the judge sentence you to two years in prison. But you didn't do it. You passed a lie detector test, and your accuser has changed her story three times. If you do two years in prison, you will lose your job. So you take it to the box. You are found guilty. The judge sentences you to 11 years in prison. End of real-life example.

There are several methods of evaluating the "take-the-plea-deal or don't-take-the-plea-deal" decision. Some methods are mathematical. Some are not. Always evaluate it mathematically first. You can use alternative methods afterwards.

14.1. Mathematical analysis

Imagine that you are the guy in the real-life example above. Imagine that the trial has not yet started. The prosecutor offers you two years and you're facing a maximum of twelve. Should you accept the offer and plead guilty? There are two critical things that you don't know: 1) will you win or lose at trial? and 2) how long a prison sentence will you receive from the judge if you lose? You are facing what scientists and economists call a "decision under uncertainty." There are techniques from the fields of game theory, risk management, and statistics that have been developed to help you with this. The first step is to assign probabilities to your unknowns (probabilities just means percentages).

14.2. Probability of Winning at Trial

This is the most important unknown. If you were to look up the outcome of every criminal trial that has happened in every courtroom in America over the last 20 years, you would find that the defendant walked away with a not-guilty-on-all-counts verdict less than 10 percent of the time. Far less. We'll use 5 percent as our first estimate.

14.3. Expected Length of Sentence if Found Guilty

Judges hate trials and want every defendant to take a plea. This is true in both federal and state courts, but a little bit more so in state courts. So, if you are found guilty at trial, the judge will give you the longest sentence he can, or close to it, simply to punish you for not accepting a plea. That judge will use you to send a message to every defendant in the country who might be considering going to trial: you had better take the prosecution's plea offer because I will bury you if you don't. Remember, judges don't really care whether you're innocent or guilty. All they care about is that there is not a long backlog of cases piling up in their courtrooms. If you take a plea deal, that keeps the traffic flowing smoothly through their courtroom. If you don't, then traffic backs up for miles behind you like when your car breaks down on a busy highway.

This leads to the following perverse outcome: the innocent are punished more harshly than the guilty. This is so because guilty people are less averse to admitting their guilt and taking the plea deal. For this they are rewarded with shorter sentences. Innocent people are less inclined to plead guilty and thus more likely to go to trial where they are usually found guilty and punished with longer prison sentences.

For our example, we'll use the maximum, 12 years, as the expected sentence if found guilty at trial. Next, we will multiply all the probabilities and all the sentence lengths together to generate expectations for taking the plea and not taking the plea.[19] Then we can compare the two.

If you plead guilty: you will receive a 2-year prison sentence.

If you go to trial and win: you walk. Zero years in prison.

If you go to trial and lose: you'll receive a 12-year prison sentence.

Your expected sentence if you choose to go to trial:

5% chance of winning x 0 years if you win

---

[19] This comes from Von Neumann, J. and Morganstern, O. *Theory of Games and Economic Behavior* (1944).

+   95% chance of losing x 12 years if you lose

=   expected sentence of 11.4 years in prison

Now compare: 11.4 years if you go to trial > two years if you plead guilty. You'll probably wind up getting 11.4 years if you go to trial. You'll probably get two years if you plead guilty. You are better off pleading guilty and it's not a close call.

So, our first look at the mathematical analysis tells us very strongly that we should plead guilty. But there are many more questions to be addressed, so let's keep analyzing.

"Didn't you say in an earlier chapter that the judge doesn't have to give me the sentence that the prosecutor recommends? So why are you using the prosecutor's recommendation in your analysis?"

Right you are. In our example, you pled guilty to a third-degree felony, so the judge could choose to sentence you to the statutory maximum which is five years. So if we now recompute: you still expect to get 11.4 years if you go to trial. However, you now expect to get five years from the judge if you plead guilty. Five years is still way better than 11.4 years so you're still way better off pleading guilty.

"You got your probability of winning at trial by looking at all the trials in all the courtrooms in America over the past 20 years. Lots of those defendants were probably guilty. I'm innocent! And I'm sure I can win at trial."

Ooh! You had me until that last sentence. Innocent defendants are found guilty at trial all the time. I've seen estimates that 100,000 to 200,000 people currently in prison are innocent out of a total nationwide prison population of roughly 2 million. (America has more people locked up than any other nation on earth.) "The Innocence Project" has exonerated quite a few people on death row using DNA evidence. There are still more who are innocent but have no way to prove it because there is no DNA evidence in their case.

There is simply no way to know with any certainty the percentage of innocent defendants who take their cases to trial and are found guilty. So let's just plug in some rough guesses and see what the numbers tell us. Let's start with 50 percent; that's always a sensible first guess when you have no idea what the true percentage is. What if innocent defendants are found guilty 50 percent of the time and not guilty 50 percent of the time? In that case, the expected outcome for the (so he claims) innocent defendant in our real-world example is a prison sentence of 50% x 12 years = 6 years. Compare that to his plea offer of two years. He is still better off taking the deal and pleading guilty. Let's try another rough guess. What if innocent defendants are found not guilty at trial 80 percent of the time and found guilty 20 percent of the time? In that case his expected sentence is 20% x 12 years = 2.4 years. 2.4 years is still worse than what the prosecution is offering, so he should probably still take the deal and plead guilty. It turns out that the break-even point happens at 2 years / 12 years = 16.66 percent. So if you believe you have only a 16.66 percent chance of losing and a (100 - 16.66 =) 83.34 percent chance of winning, and you are willing to gamble 10 years of your life, then you should consider going to trial.

Actually, no, you should still take the plea offer. Because, if you've never been to trial before, you still do not fully comprehend how badly biased criminal trials are against the defendant. Even after reading this whole book twice from cover to cover, you still cannot appreciate how many ways they've tilted the playing field against you and in favor of the prosecution, so your estimate of winning your trial 83.34 percent of the time is almost certainly way too optimistic. Furthermore, if you're innocent, you still have not accepted down deep in your heart that nobody in that courtroom but you gives a shit. You may be telling yourself that you understand this, but your understanding is superficial. Down deep, a part of you still clings to the belief that the American criminal justice system is designed to convict the guilty and exonerate the innocent. Nope. The system is designed to convict everybody, innocent and guilty alike. So your estimate of having an 83.34 percent chance of winning at trial is way too optimistic.

All of the above analysis applies to regular people. If you are very, very rich, you might consider ignoring everything I just wrote and taking your case to trial. How rich? If you can drop $500,000 to $1,000,000 on your defense, you might have a chance to win. You'll need a team of expensive lawyers and lots of independent expert witnesses and private investigators to collect and analyze evidence. You can't win if the police collect all the evidence, county coroners and forensic examiners who are hired by the prosecution and work with the police do all the analysis, and then prosecutors decide what evidence will and what evidence won't be shown to the jury. Fighting back against all that costs a lot of money. You are fighting against the government. They have unlimited resources to use against you. The aphorism that it's better to be rich and guilty than poor and innocent is true.

What if you are so poor that you couldn't make bail when you were first arraigned? Let's suppose that you sat in county jail for eight months before the prosecution came to you with their offer of two years. If you plead guilty, you will get credit for the eight months you spent in jail already; you only have to serve an additional 16 months in prison. If you go to trial and lose, you still get the eight months credit; you have to serve an additional 11 years and four months in prison. Now compare 16 months (16 months equals 1.33 years) if you plead guilty to an expected sentence of 11.4

years minus the eight months you served in county jail (11.4 years minus eight months equals 11.4 - 0.66 years equals 10.74 years). Your new break-even point is 1.33 years / 10.74 years equals 12.38 percent. You need to believe you have an 87.62 percent chance to win at trial and only a 12.38 percent chance to lose before you should consider going to trial.

Over and over, when you analyze the decision mathematically using statistics and expected values, the numbers tell you the same thing: plead guilty. Take the deal. But statistics and quantitative analysis are not the be all and end all. There are non-mathematical considerations, too. Let's look at some of those.

First, be aware that, in order to get the deal that they are offering, you have to plead guilty. When you plead guilty, they're going to make you stand up in court and say out loud that you did whatever they say you did and that you are very, very, very sorry you did it.[20] After your coerced apology, the judge will swell with patrician pride and sanctimony before making a short speech for the benefit of any newspaper reporters or voting-age citizens who happen to be present in the courtroom telling them what a very, very, very bad person you are for having done the things that you just pled guilty to doing. Then he will sentence you.

Some people claim that they refused to plead guilty because they simply would not have been able to live with themselves had they lied and said they did something they didn't do. This is a self-serving rationalization coming from someone who refused all his plea offers, went to trial and lost. But if their story is true then I respect their decision.

---

[20] There is an exception to this called an "Alford" plea. But I'm not going to get into that.

I remember meeting a Mexican guy whose English was not very good. He was guilty and willing to admit it. But, over the course of the plea negotiations, his lawyer had gotten the prosecution to drop the charges he was actually guilty of and now wanted him to plead guilty to lesser charges for things he had not actually done. He kept telling his lawyer that he couldn't plead guilty to those things because he hadn't done them. His lawyer became annoyed and said, "It doesn't matter! Just plead guilty to these charges and say you're sorry!" The Mexican guy replied, "My mother and father never taught me how to lie so good. You tell the prosecutor and judge to write down on a piece of paper what they want me to say, and I will read it word for word."

Second, you should be aware that if you plead guilty you pretty much forfeit all your rights to appeal. That's another reason that they want you to take a plea deal so badly: it reduces the burden on the appellate courts. Technically, you could still be allowed to appeal. But first you have to file a "motion to withdraw guilty plea" with the court. Almost nobody ever wins those. So, once you say you did it, you did it.

Third, perhaps your situation is such that two years in prison will mean losing your job, your career, access to your children, your home, or some other intolerable outcome. There are many important factors that might lead you to a jury trial even though the numbers clearly say that pleading guilty would be the better move. Only you know your situation. I leave all those considerations to you.

The bottom line is this. If your objective is to minimize the length of time that you spend in prison, then you should plead guilty, and it does not matter whether you are factually guilty or innocent.

This conclusion leads to some sickening and ironic implications. For example, it implies that defense lawyers may be right to just shepherd every client they represent towards taking a deal and pleading guilty. It doesn't justify the lying and false displays of bravado that take place in the early stages of every case. It doesn't justify the continued lying about all the preparation for trial and poring through evidence that lawyers pretend to have done until their clients have run out of money. But perhaps it does justify the fact that they never really intended to take the case to trial.

If they could just be honest with their clients and tell them that the system is stacked too heavily against them to merit putting up much of a fight, that the best course of action is to plead guilty, then everyone might be better off. Defendants would be disgruntled, sure - but they would receive shorter prison sentences and spend less money. Courtrooms would be less busy; jails would be less crowded; and the criminal justice system as a whole would be less clogged. That would make judges and county sheriffs happy. Prosecutors would get the convictions they crave and do much less work. That makes them happy. Defense attorneys would make less money, but they would work less and live a far more honest existence. But America as a country would suffer. America would have to abandon the pretenses that every citizen is entitled to their day in court, that all American citizens receive equal justice and due process of law, and that our justice system is the envy of every other nation on earth.

Chapter 15: Jury Selection

Eventually, they'll run out of continuances and the day will come when they have to start your trial. Often, but not always, the prosecution will make last-minute plea offers that are more attractive than earlier offers in order to induce you to plead guilty. Your lawyer will almost certainly put a little extra pressure on you to take these offers, partly because he has been putting off preparing for trial this whole time and, if you take a plea, he's off the hook. He may tell you that these new offers are fantastically generous, and he will stress the maximum prison sentence you could receive if you are found guilty of all charges. But if you decide to turn down these offers, trial begins.

The first step is to select the jury. The legal name for this is "voir dire," an old French term roughly equivalent to "show and tell" or "to tell the truth." We'll just call it jury selection.

Jury selection works like this: they bring in a large group of people - between 75 and 100 regular citizens who have been chosen for jury duty. Of those, they need to find 16 who are acceptable to sit on your jury (16 = 12 regular jurors + 4 alternate jurors). The judge will tell the large group of jurors when he expects the trial to start and how long he expects it to last. (After telling the jurors this, I have seen judges look to the prosecutor and ask, "Right?" the prosecutor replies, "that's right, your honor." The judges never asked the defense attorneys how long the trial will take, only the prosecutors.) Any potential juror who cannot be available for the entirety of the trial gets excused. The remaining jurors get a questionnaire to fill out and then get sent home and told to come back Monday (or whenever).

The questionnaires are comprised of personal questions designed to help the lawyers select the best jurors and weed out the worst ones. These questions will include, "Have you ever served on a jury before?" "Have you ever been convicted of a crime?" "How many years of schooling have you completed?" "What is your race?" "Is English your first language?" "Are you or any members of your immediate family on the police force?" etc.

These questionnaires are supposed to be designed jointly by the prosecution and the defense. What this means in practice is that the questionnaire is written entirely by the prosecutor and the defense attorney looks at it for five seconds and says, "Yep, that looks fine."

Next, the remaining pool of eligible jurors (also called the "venire") returns and sits in the courtroom. They are then called upon in a random order to be interviewed by the prosecution and defense. During these interviews, the lawyers from each side will flatter, praise, and glorify each juror in order to win their favor before trial. To me it seems completely phony and obvious, but the jurors seem to like it. It's sad to think that an innocent defendant could get the death penalty because the prosecutor is better at buttering up the jury than the defense attorney is.

After these interviews, the prosecutors and defense lawyers, separately, can decide whether to strike or allow each juror to serve. Each side is given a limited number of peremptory strikes, which means they can strike a potential juror from the panel without a reason. The rest of the strikes require a reason.

In 1985 there was a famous U.S. Supreme Court case called Batson v. Kentucky where the defendant was a black man, and the prosecutor used all four of his allotted peremptory challenges to strike all four of the minority persons on the venire. Batson's lawyer objected, but the trial judge overruled the objection, saying that peremptory challenges could be used for any reason. Batson appealed to the appellate court. Lost. Took it to the state Supreme Court. Lost. Managed to get his case accepted by the U.S. Supreme

Court. The Supreme Court sided with Batson, writing, "A state denies a black defendant equal protection of the laws when it puts him on trial before a jury from which members of his race have been purposefully excluded."

Books have been written about how to gain the upper hand at trial through superior selection of jurors.[21] There are television shows about it. In the movie "Runaway Jury," Gene Hackman plays a high-priced jury selection consultant who claims to be able to win trials for his rich corporate clients with his sophisticated juror profiling techniques.

Here is my opinion: if you are the defendant, you want the smartest people you can get on your jury. If you are the prosecutor, you want the dumbest. It's as simple as that. Smart people actually spend time and mental energy thinking about what "beyond a reasonable doubt" means. Dumb people tend to say, "Well, I think he's guilty. So I'm voting guilty. Let's go home." Smart people occasionally think for themselves. Dumb people tend to say, "Well, everyone else seems to think he's guilty; so I guess I think he's guilty, too." And more than anything else, dumb people just want an authority figure to tell them how to think. They are going to fall in line behind the prosecutor because he is more authoritative, more competent, better prepared, and more confident than the defense attorney.

But what if you're guilty? Won't the smarter people be more likely to figure this out than the dumber people? Maybe, but it doesn't matter. The effect of this is negligible. The only thing that really matters is that the dumb people are

---

[21] I have read two of these books, and they were, if not completely worthless, about as close as you could get to worthless without falling in.

going to do whatever the prosecutor tells them to do without really thinking about it.

With all that in mind, here is a piece of very bad news for defendants: jury selection is inherently biased towards selecting dumb people and against selecting smart people. Why? Because anybody that has an important job gets excused from jury duty. If you are a doctor and your patients need you, you are excused. If you are a computer network specialist and your company needs you, you are excused. If you're a teacher, a plumber, an accountant, or the CEO of a small business, you are excused. But if you are unemployed? Welcome to the jury. Remember this: a jury is made up of 12 people who were too stupid to get out of jury duty.[22]

A brief aside: I don't know how the original venire is chosen. I would assume people in the community are randomly selected and mailed summonses. But is it really random? Could the court, maybe when a police officer is on trial for murder, pack the venire with confederates who will not return a guilty verdict no matter what? How do we know it's all fair and above board? We don't.

---

[22] An old joke. I don't know where it's from. My apologies to its author.

Chapter 16: Trial

When you walk into the courtroom, you will see at the front of the room a judge sitting at a raised platform with the state seal, state flag, and state motto on the wall behind him. Near the judge's platform will be the witness box and a small desk for the stenographer. Next you will see two tables, one for the prosecution and one for the defense. Behind these two tables are rows of benches or chairs, divided into two sides by an aisleway. One side is for the prosecution and friends of the victim. The other side is for the defense and friends of the defendant.

Many people have the misconception that the judge acts as a referee during the trial, similar to a referee at a basketball or football game, blowing the whistle when either side commits a foul, and then imposing the appropriate penalty. But that's not how it works. The judge won't do anything at all unless a lawyer raises an objection. The judge will then either sustain the objection or overrule it. But if you have a lawyer who never objects, then the prosecutor will take from you every right you think you have, and the judge won't do a damned thing about it. And that is, in fact, what happens. Defense attorneys don't like to object to things that prosecutors do. When they object, the prosecutors scowl at them. And, as we know, defense attorneys are far more interested in toadying up to prosecutors than in defending their clients' constitutional rights. So, it is at trial that most defendants learn that the rights that they had previously believed to be inalienable vaporize when they are needed most.

People who have never been to trial don't understand this, especially the talking heads on television, many of whom have been to law school. They think that if the constitution says that everybody has a right not to be searched unreasonably, then you actually have a right not to be searched unreasonably; and if it says that everybody has a right to due process of law before being deprived of life, liberty, or property, then you actually have a right to due process of law.

Instead, think of your rights as something similar to speed limits on highways. The sign might say that the speed limit is 55 mph. But when you look out your window at the other cars, you see that none of them are going slower than 70 mph, and some of them are doing over 90. Rarely does anybody get pulled over and ticketed.

If someone were to say to me, "People don't drive over 55 mph on the Pennsylvania Turnpike," I would reply, "Yes they do. I've driven on the Pennsylvania Turnpike many times and everybody drives that fast or faster." If the person then said, "No, they don't. See? The sign says the speed limit is 55 mph." I would think to myself, "This person is an idiot," and I would say out loud, "Well, you've obviously never actually driven on the Pennsylvania Turnpike, because nobody obeys those signs."

I feel the same way about people who say that everybody has a right to a fair trial, or that American citizens have constitutional rights to confront their accusers, equal protection of the laws, and protection against unreasonable searches and seizures. I think to myself, "this person is an idiot who has obviously never been to trial before."

On television, when a news anchor needs answers to questions about the criminal justice system, the screen splits in half and a subject matter expert appears for the news anchor to interview. The subject matter expert is always a former prosecutor or judge or a retired police chief. But if you truly want to understand how justice is administered in this country, these are precisely the wrong people to ask. These people are wealthy and powerful members of the class that is responsible for the maintenance of the unfairness that now exists.

In order for you to have, in any way that one might consider meaningful, constitutional rights at trial, it is necessary that your lawyer object when those rights are violated.[23] You cannot count on him to do this, of course, for all the normal reasons: laziness, incompetence, apathy, lack of preparation, and obsequiousness to the prosecutor.

I have read the transcripts of quite a few trials. Generally, I keep count as I read of the number of objections raised by the prosecution and by the defense. Usually - not always, but usually - the prosecutor objects three, four, or five times as often as the defense attorney. To me, this is a clear sign that the prosecutor wants to win and the defense attorney doesn't really care.

One could argue that the relative lack of defense objections is caused not by the defense attorney's laziness, but by the extreme scrupulousness and professionalism of the prosecutor: there is simply nothing for the defense attorney to object to. But, come on. Who are we kidding here? Prosecutors care only about winning and they are quite willing to play dirty if that is what it takes to win. I hold this truth to be self-evident.

In case you are curious, the defendant is not allowed to object at trial. Only the lawyer is. So, if he fails to protect you and then you object in order to defend your rights, the judge will hold you in contempt of court. It's quite frustrating for knowledgeable defendants.

A similar frustration arises when you watch your lawyer bungle the cross-examination of witnesses. It frequently happens that witnesses do not tell the truth under oath. Sometimes they flat-out lie. Sometimes they remember

---

[23] Your lawyer's failure to object at trial actually does more damage to your chances on appeal then at trial. Much more on this in later chapters.

102

things wrongly. Sometimes they make up answers when they really ought to say, "I'm sorry. I don't know." Often, you the defendant know that they are lying. You know most of the witnesses. They are generally asked questions about things that they did with you or for you. So, you know when they are lying. But your lawyer, who is the one standing at the front of the courtroom cross-examining them, has no idea. There is no way for you, the defendant, to get your lawyer to ask the right questions and expose the witnesses' lies. You can't stop the trial.

For example, imagine that the witness says under oath that she had never, ever seen you before the night that the crime occurred. You know that she's lying and you can prove it. You had talked to her at parties around town several times before and you have at least one photograph on your Facebook page where the two of you are standing right next to each other. Your lawyer is completely unaware of this, so he just lets these lies slip by completely unchallenged.

And then these lies become the truth. When you appeal your conviction, the prosecution will write in their opposition to your appeal brief that the witness had never seen you before in her life. Then you will write in your response brief, "She was lying and I have photographic evidence that proves it." You may even include the printouts of the Facebook photos to prove to the appellate court that what you are saying is true.

It won't matter. The appellate judges[24] will say, "The appellant is talking nonsense! The witness said under oath that she had never seen him before." Then they will quote the line in the trial transcript where she said so. "It is the job

---

[24] Appellate judges are mostly former prosecutors. A few are former corporate lawyers. Defense attorneys very rarely get chosen for this job.

of the jury, not the appellate court, to determine which witnesses are being truthful and which are lying. If the witness lied, appellant had ample opportunity to demonstrate that to the jury at trial." Finally, they will say that your Facebook photos are inadmissible on appeal because they are not part of the trial record.

And that witness' lie, provably false, will remain the truth for all eternity. Decades later, when you see the parole board, if you say to them, "She was lying and I can prove it," they will respond, "He refuses to accept responsibility for his actions," and deny parole.

The problem is just as bad when your lawyer is questioning expert witnesses. Expert witnesses include coroners, medical examiners, doctors, graphologists, computer forensics specialists, ballistics experts, etc. Each one of these experts gets paid by the prosecution to appear and testify at your trial. Most of them have worked with the police and prosecutors many times before. They have helped convict many defendants before you. Imagine the opposite for a second: imagine the forensics expert's testimony had helped to exonerate many defendants before you. The prosecutors would simply stop hiring that guy and shop around for a forensics expert who gets them the results they want. They want convictions. So, they find forensics experts who give testimony that leads to convictions.

The way that you, the defendant, can combat this is by hiring your own forensics experts. This costs a lot of money and takes time. And those are two things that all defense attorneys hate to spend: money and time. So, your attorney is just going to cross examine the prosecution's expert witnesses. If you complain that you want your own experts, he will tell you that he spoke to several non-prosecution experts and they all gave the same answers as the prosecution's expert, so there really would be no point in hiring one of them. But that is a lie.

Some expert witnesses are not really experts at all. Take the county coroner, for example. They don't need to have a medical degree. In most counties, they are elected officials. They are politicians, not doctors. In some counties the sheriff is the coroner.

What if you catch one lying or making a mistake? Imagine that you are a defendant who has a medical degree. Imagine that the coroner gives sworn testimony on the witness stand that is plainly wrong. For instance, he states with great confidence and authority that rigor mortis[25] does not begin to set in until at least 12 hours after death. You went to medical school and know that that is not the case. Your lawyer should rip him apart on cross examination, but he refuses to. He seems more concerned with not embarrassing the coroner than with proving your innocence. So, what can you do? Can you question the coroner yourself? After all, you know more about rigor mortis than your lawyer or the judge, and it's your life that's on the line. But the answer is no, you cannot. Only the lawyer may question the witness. You will be held in contempt if you try to.

Also, all your knowledge and medical training will be ignored because you are the defendant. It will be assumed

---

[25] Rigor mortis: n. The rigidity or stiffening of the muscles, and hence the body, after death. It is due chiefly to an accumulation of lactic acid in the muscle tissue. The rapidity of onset and the duration of rigidity vary with the condition of the muscles prior to death, as with regard to activity, with the temperature of the environment, and other factors. The onset is from 1 to 7 hours after death. The disappearance is from one to five days. Rigor mortis begins with the muscles of the jaws, and progresses from the head down, to the legs and feet.—from "The Attorneys' Dictionary of Medicine."

that everything you say is inherently untrustworthy, that you are simply making statements in your own interest.

This is a bias built into the legal system. Statements in your own interest are never believed by the court and statements against interest are always believed. Here is the legal definition:

Statement against interest: a statement that was at the time of its making so far contrary to the declarant's pecuniary or proprietary interest, or so far tended to subject the defendant to civil or criminal liability, or to render invalid a claim by the declarant against another that a reasonable person in the declarant's position would not have made it.

When the police first bring a suspect in for questioning it is quite common for him to deny any involvement in the crime and to deny any knowledge of the crime. Then the police collect more evidence and question more witnesses, so they decide to bring the suspect - let's call him Cody - in for a second round of questioning. During this second round, Cody changes his story. He now says he does know about the crime. He wasn't there when it happened, but he has talked to a lot of people and the "word on the street" is that you (he gives the police your name) were the main perpetrator. There may have been some other people involved; he's not sure. The police then collect more evidence and question more witnesses, so they decide to bring Cody in for a third round of questioning. During this third round, he changes his story again: yes, he was there at the crime scene; yes, he participated in the crime, but it wasn't his idea; it was your idea; you thought the whole thing up; you practically had to twist his arm to get him to go along with it and to keep quiet afterwards.

Now, the police say to him, "we're going to give you a choice. You either testify in court to what you just said, or we are going to charge you with aggravated burglary and felony murder with the possibility of the death penalty," so Cody agrees to plead guilty and testify against you.[26] He is now cooperating with the prosecution. He has "flipped."

Soon, the prosecution will make him sign a contract agreeing to tell them everything he knows. These contracts are completely one-sided. Here is an example:

"Should it be judged by the prosecutor's office at any time that the defendant has failed to cooperate fully, refused to testify or testifies falsely in any proceeding(s), has intentionally given false, misleading, or incomplete information or testimony, or has otherwise violated any provision of this agreement, then the prosecutor's office may automatically reinstate the original charges against the defendant as well as file any additional charges."

If the prosecution decides for any reason that they feel Cody is not being completely truthful with them, then they are freed from any promises they made. So, in practice, it is a contract that Cody cannot get out of, but the prosecution can get out of it whenever they please. They are not bound by it at all unless they choose to be.

Once this contract has been signed, the more information Cody gives the prosecution that helps them convict you, the happier the prosecutors will be with him; And the more information he gives them that exculpates you and makes the task of convicting you more difficult, the more censorious they will be with him. They will frequently remind him that he will get the death penalty if he does not tell them what they have already decided is the truth. So, he will tell them. And he will lie to make them happy. The fact that Cody is lying won't really matter. Everything he says that helps the prosecution, whether false or true, will be

---

[26] "A man can't be too careful in his choice of enemies"—Oscar Wilde

called a "statement against interest." This ambiguous little phrase will wash away every sin that Cody has ever committed for that brief moment that he is testifying against you. The obvious notion that statements that were against interest prior to flipping and cooperating become statements in his self-interest after flipping is completely foreign to the criminal justice system, in practice. The definition of "statement against interest" includes the qualifying condition, "at the time of its making," but that is ignored.

Occasionally, you'll hear television pundits talking with "legal analysts" about a high-profile criminal investigation after the FBI has flipped a key witness. The pundit will point out that the newly flipped witness has "credibility issues" because he is a confessed criminal and an admitted liar. The legal analyst will then say, "Yes, that's true. But the prosecution isn't going to trial on this witness testimony alone. There is going to be corroborating evidence."

The part about corroborating evidence is usually true, but the part about "credibility issues" is laughable. Convicting people based on the testimony of lying criminals is a *sine qua non* of federal prosecutions. The FBI's entire business model consists of catching low level criminals in the act and then pressuring them to flip and testify against people higher up the food chain. If juries didn't credit the testimony of witnesses who had agreed to testify in exchange for lighter sentences, federal prosecutors would never manage to convict anybody. In reality, their conviction rate is extremely high. So "credibility issues" are not a hindrance at all.

Incidentally, they can convict you based on the testimony of a single witness with no corroborating evidence. Juries are given the following instruction before they retire to deliberate:

"You may believe or disbelieve all or any part of the testimony of any witness. It is your province to determine what testimony is worthy of belief and what testimony is not worthy of belief. The testimony of one witness, if believed by you, is sufficient to prove any fact."

So, if the witness says he saw you commit the crime and the jury chooses to believe his testimony, that proves that you are guilty.

Defense attorneys don't work very hard to expose the lies and inconsistencies in the testimony of the prosecution's cooperating witnesses, either. It's too hard and too time-consuming. In the previous example, Cody was interviewed by the police three separate times: twice before he agreed to cooperate, and once after. These interviews were all recorded. Later, they are transcribed and typed up. Let's say the first interview is 35 pages long, the second is 28 pages, and the third is 55 pages. That makes 118 pages total. Let's say that for your lawyer to read those transcripts with the attention and care necessary to identify lies and inconsistencies, he can read about 8 pages per hour. At that rate, it would take him over 13 hours to go through all three transcripts—13 hours of fairly hard work. So there is no way your lawyer is going to study those transcripts. If he tells you he did, he is lying. He skimmed them for 20 minutes at most.

Public pretenders have the built-in excuse that they are overburdened. They have about one hour per month to spend on each client they represent. Thirteen hours, then, is more than a year's worth of work on your case. Paid lawyers have the built-in excuse that it doesn't really matter because you were going to lose anyway.

When you read the transcripts of police interrogations you frequently see examples of the suspect trying to change his story.

Police: So, when you went to Xavier's apartment on the night of the 22nd, did you see the gun in his closet then?

Suspect: I wasn't at his apartment that night. I might have seen him outside Applebee's, but I wasn't...

Police: Hold on a sec. Last time you told us you did see him at his apartment. So, you were lying...

Suspect: Um, uh, no... Yeah. I did see him at his apartment. You were right. I got confused.

This sort of police technique makes it harder for suspects to lie. But it also forces suspects to maintain lies that they would prefer to correct. This is one of the ways that even guilty defendants get convicted based on lies. There are many people in prison right now who, in fact, did the crime, but most of what the jury actually heard was lies that the defense lawyer never challenged.

Having read the transcripts of many trials, I've noticed that defense lawyers spend far less time questioning witnesses than prosecutors do. I simply count the number of pages in the transcript where a witness is being examined by a prosecutor and compare that to the number of pages where the witness is being questioned by the defense lawyer. I've also noticed that when the prosecution finishes their examination and the judge asks, "Does the defense wish to cross examine?" defense counsel will say, "No questions, Your Honor. Thank you." Or "We're not going to need anything of this witness, Your Honor." Or "Just a few questions to clarify a couple of points. This is going to be very brief, Your Honor."

When a defense attorney says he's going to be very brief, he will be very brief - every time. It's not some psychological ploy designed to get the witness to let their guard down like on the TV show "Colombo." Judges are very concerned with staying on schedule and keeping all their cases moving through their courtroom. Defense attorneys know this. So they try to gain favor with the judge by keeping things brief and tidy. Maybe that judge will be appreciative and will recommend that attorney when court appointments come up in the future. Each court- appointed client means more money for the defense lawyer.

After all the witnesses have given testimony and all the evidence has been presented, three steps remain to reach the end of the trial: 1) the defendant may take the witness stand and testify in his own defense, 2) the prosecution and defense each give their closing arguments, and 3) the jury is given instructions and then retires to deliberate until it reaches a verdict. Each of these topics will be described in succeeding chapters.

Chapter 17: Judge and Jury: A Comedy of Errors

This chapter will be slightly different from the others in that the previous chapters started with a general point or thesis and supported it with case law and excerpts from trial transcripts. This chapter will start with excerpts from one particular trial and work inductively toward general propositions about the legal system. The specific errors made in this trial are not, in themselves, important, because these specific errors are not likely to arise in your trial. What is important are the generalizations about the legal system writ large that these errors illuminate and the conclusions we can infer.

The following is taken from the transcript of a murder trial. It begins with the judge reading instructions to the jury.

> Judge:[27] When you retire to the jury room, the twelve regular jurors will select a foreperson. The alternates should listen to the deliberations but not…
>
> Counsel approach.
>
> (Thereupon a sidebar was held outside the hearing of the court reporter and the jury.)
>
> Judge: I had a question about this next instruction, and counsel all agree it is appropriate. I hesitate not because I think I know more. They probably know more. But I like to make sure it is correct before I read it to you.
>
> The alternates, when you retire to the jury room, the twelve regular jurors will select a

---

[27] In actual trial transcripts, they don't call the judge "judge." They refer to him as "The Court." I prefer to use "judge."

foreperson. So the two alternates will not participate in that process. The alternates should listen to the deliberations but not participate in the deliberations, unless, until, if ever, they are called upon to serve as a regular juror. Alternate jurors were selected to serve in the event of any misfortune befalling a member of the panel. As yet, that has fortunately not occurred. Nevertheless, your presence is still required while this jury is deliberating.

After these instructions were read, the twelve regular jurors and the two alternate jurors went back to the jury room to deliberate. That is when the fun started.

During deliberations, juries are allowed to ask questions of the judge. They do this by writing their questions on paper, handing them to the bailiff,[28] who brings it to the judge, who reads the questions aloud and announces his answer. The lawyers may then object to the judge's answers before they are written down and returned to the jury, if they are unhappy with any of them.

In this trial, once the alternates and regular jurors were alone together in the jury room, they soon began to argue with each other. The first alternate wanted to get one of the regular jurors kicked off the panel so that he could replace him. So he wrote his question down on paper, gave it to the bailiff, who brought it to the judge, who read it aloud in court.

Judge: The question is, "Can a juror be removed for stating she shouldn't have been

---

[28] Bailiff: n. An officer, similar to a sheriff, employed to keep order in the court.

picked and she has trouble and doesn't like considering circumstantial evidence? [29]

I'm not positive, but I believe this question may have been written about someone else. An hour later, the bailiff brought the judge another question from the jury.

> Judge: "Can Mr. C. be accused,"[30] — I assume it means 'recused'[31] – "from the jury because it is hard for him to listen in without commenting or putting in his two sense." (sic)

> As a way of background, I believe this question is the result of the last question from the jury."

So first Mr. C, an alternate, tried to get one of the regular jurors kicked out so that he could take their place. Then, the regular jurors got fed up with Mr. C. and tried to get him kicked out.

It turns out that none of this is legal. Alternates are prohibited from being in the jury room during deliberations. It is completely against the rules of court and a violation of the defendant's constitutional right to a trial by an impartial jury. This all derives from the Sixth Amendment, so let's start there.

---

[29] Circumstantial evidence will be explained at the end of this chapter.
[30] They used the alternate's full name. I shortened it to "Mr. C."
[31] Accuse: v. To charge with fault, offense, or crime. Recuse: v. To reject or challenge a judge or juror disqualified to act.

17.1. Amendment VI

In all criminal prosecutions, the accused shall enjoy[32] the right to a speedy and public trial, by an impartial jury of the state and district wherein the crime shall have been committed, which district shall have previously ascertained by law, and to be informed of the nature and cause of the accusation; to be confronted with the witnesses against him; to have compulsory process for obtaining witnesses in his favor, and to have the Assistance of Counsel for his defense."

The key part of the Sixth Amendment, for our purposes, is the word "impartial." The United States' Supreme Court has interpreted this word to mean "free from outside influences."

"A fair trial can be achieved only if the jury is insulated from outside communications or influences.

"The inviolability of the jury room from outside influences, actual or potential, is a prime necessity in the administration of justice."[33]

Alternate jurors are considered outside influences once the jury retires to deliberate:

---

[32] I'm not sure I would have chosen the word "enjoy" had I been a framer of the Constitution. That may have been a good time for ol' James Madison to have reached for his thesaurus.

[33] In re Murchison (1955).

"The alternate then became as any other stranger to the proceedings regardless of whether she had been discharged. Thus, the alternate was as any other outsider would have been when she continued to sit with the jurors as they began their own proceedings."[34]

Not only the U.S. Supreme Court, but the State Supreme Court where this trial took place, too, had repeatedly held that it is error for an alternate to be permitted to sit in during jury deliberations even if given instructions not to participate in the deliberations:

"The trial court clearly erred in allowing the alternate jurors to remain present during deliberations."[35]

"Allowing alternate jurors to be present during jury deliberations violates the sanctity of the jury process."[36]

So, sending alternate jurors to sit with regular jurors is error. That is completely clear. The State Supreme Court said so, as did the U.S. Supreme Court.

Here is my first question: how on earth did the judge not know this? Not only the judge, but the prosecutor and the defense attorney all had a little conference out of earshot of the jury,[37] the defendant, and the rest of the courtroom, where they unanimously agreed that it's fine for alternates and regular jurors to deliberate together. Had none of them

---

[34] United States v. Beasley (1972).

[35] Ohio v. Jackson (2001).

[36] Ohio v. Murphy (2001).

[37] It is also against the rules for judges and lawyers to have these unrecorded sidebars. This will be discussed at the end of this chapter.

ever conducted an actual jury trial before? Every trial has both regular and alternate jurors. How could a supposedly experienced judge not know where alternate jurors belong when trial finishes and deliberations begin? This judge actually had an inkling that something might be amiss. That's why he had counsel approach. I'm not sure whether that makes it better or worse. Is it worse to entirely overlook an error or to notice it and then decide, "No, that's perfectly alright"? The former could be explained by carelessness; the latter clearly demonstrates that the judge does not know the law. It's like skipping a problem on a test as opposed to attempting it and getting the answer completely wrong. The former could be carelessness, but the latter shows you don't know the subject.

If I were to tell you that I just watched an NFL football game in which none of the referees knew how many yards a delay of game penalty was worth, you'd probably reply, "I don't believe you. NFL refs are highly trained professionals doing an important job. It's impossible for one experienced ref to not know something that fundamental, let alone three." But here we have the criminal justice system equivalent: the judge and two lawyers all got together, and nobody knew where the alternate jurors were supposed to go. I probably wouldn't have believed it myself were it not all recorded and documented in the trial transcript. Judges and prosecutors are paid a lot of money, and that money comes from taxpayers. One would think that taxpayers would prefer not to be paying for incompetent job performance.

How is this whole thing even possible? One reason is that hardly any criminal cases go to trial. Nowadays they all get decided by plea. So judges and lawyers don't actually have as much experience with trials as they pretend. That is another reason that they all want the defendant to plead guilty so badly. I have written about how costly and time-consuming trials are, and how this makes courts want to avoid them. But trials are also opportunities for judges and lawyers to make mistakes and look stupid. Mistakes may happen when lawyers get together to negotiate the terms of a plea bargain, but those meetings take place behind closed doors and are not recorded. Trials, on the other hand, are public and recorded. Those blunders are preserved and live on forever.

Be aware that not every lawyer is good at his job. Exactly half of them were not in the top half of their respective classes in law school. The ones that did finish near the top tend to go where the money is: corporate law, contract law, constitutional law. There is far less money to be made in criminal law. Of that money, prosecutors make more, and defense attorneys make less. So defense attorneys tend to be the bottom of the barrel. Remember also that the defense lawyer has been projecting a false confidence since the case began. He exaggerates his chances of winning at trial first to attract clients; and then, once he's gotten the client, in order to bluff the prosecutor and get better plea offers. Defense attorneys are living a lie, and this must be very stressful for them. Every trial is an opportunity for the truth to be revealed, which they want to avoid. You never see this aspect of the criminal justice system on TV shows like "LA Law," "Law and Order," or "Perry Mason." Judges may occasionally be portrayed as mean or unethical, but never incompetent. And on shows like "Judge Judy" and "the People's Court," they're portrayed as almost omniscient and infallible at law.

Another thing to point out is that the instructions the judge read after the sidebar contained the following: "the alternates should listen to the deliberations but not participate in the deliberations....," which was obviously ignored and violated by the jurors. The U.S. legal system is built on the presumption that juries follow the instructions that they are given by judges. But juries violate their instructions all the time. All the time. This presumption is based not on evidence or history but on necessity. The legal system could not function without it. For this reason, the presumption is defended like religious dogma. Those who challenge it are first laughed at, and if they persist, excommunicated and banished.

The United States Supreme Court has said the same thing, albeit much more diplomatically:

> "The rule that juries are presumed to follow their instructions is a pragmatic one, rooted less in the absolute certitude that the presumption is true than the belief that it represents a reasonable, practical accommodation of the interests of the state and the defendant."[38]

What is this "practical accommodation" they speak of: 99 percent state, 1 percent defendant? How does this rule benefit defendants at all? I don't see it. Whenever courts make pseudo-mathematical claims about "costs and benefits," "tradeoffs," or "the interests of society," you can be sure that they are trying to conceal the arbitrariness of a decision or interpretation. Courts affect pretenses of dispassionate analysis of legal questions, when what they actually do is rationalize the facts to conform to their own interests. And people spend years in prison as a result of these presumptions that even the Supreme Court has admitted aren't really true.

---

[38] Richardson v. March (1987).

But back to our jury deliberations, the alternates and the regular jurors are on the brink of war. So the judge decides to address the problem.

> Judge: So we're now back with that question. We do have a juror that's, I think, problematic. However, with the agreement of counsel, I will bring [Mr. C.] back in and express to him the importance of being an alternate, how important an alternate is to making sure that we have a full jury, how he said he would follow the law, and see if we can't get him to participate by sitting there. Do you have any objection?
>
> Prosecutor: No, Your Honor.
>
> Judge: If I do that?
>
> Prosecutor: No, I would prefer you do because I'm worried about losing the alternate.[39]
>
> Defense: No objection, Your Honor.

Notice that whenever the judge asks a question, the prosecutor answers first and defense counsel answers second. Defense counsel wouldn't want to answer first and risk having the prosecutor contradict or disagree with him. I realize that I am presenting you with only one example, but it is, in fact, part of a broader pattern.

Next, they summoned the alternate juror, Mr. C., and told him to go back to the jury room. But this time, make

---

[39] Can we infer from this answer that the prosecution is confident that they will win? The trial is over. The jury is deliberating. If the prosecution felt they were losing, would they be worried about losing the alternate?

122

sure that he does not participate in deliberations. Nobody is yet aware that alternates are not allowed to be there while the regular jurors deliberate. The prosecution even says they prefer it because they're "worried about losing the alternate." Defense counsel is also completely clueless and says, "No objection, Your Honor."

That afternoon, the alternate returned to the jury room and deliberations resumed. At 6:00 pm the jury retired for the evening without reaching a verdict.

The next morning, it became known that allowing alternate jurors to be present during deliberations is a violation of state law. Although it was not stated explicitly, there are multiple hints in the transcript that make clear that the prosecutor checked the rules of court and case law overnight and discovered the error. Defense attorneys almost never go home at night and read case law. That's too much like homework for them, and if they liked doing homework, they wouldn't have ended up at the bottom of their law school classes. The prosecutor informed the judge of the error they had made. They then had to decide what should be done.

There are basically two choices in situations such as this: declare a mistrial or try to correct the error with a "curative" instruction. This judge desperately wants to avoid a mistrial. The trial had been going on for about two weeks. Most trials only last two or three days. Trials are very expensive and judges dread falling behind schedule. So this judge will do everything in his power to come up with a curative instruction. The judge returned to the bench and spoke on the record.

> Judge: Since that time, it's come to everyone's attention that I was right, that the alternates should not be back there.

And that's not the issue; it's how to remedy the issue. The suggestion is that we bring the jury back, advise them that the alternates should not have been back, sequester the alternates separately, and tell the jury to continue deliberations, start the deliberations over with the same instructions.

Does the state agree with that remedy?

Prosecutor: Yes, Your Honor.

Judge: Does the defense agree with that remedy?

Defense: Yes, Your Honor.

Judge: [Defense Counsel], we pulled you in rather quickly. You've not had an opportunity to discuss the court's remedy either with your client, so if you need a few minutes to do that…

The judge begins with, "It's come to everyone's attention that I was right." That's clearly very important to him. But he wasn't right. He merely hesitated. That's different from being right.

As for the erroneous jury instruction, clearly the prosecutor and the judge were discussing the problem before defense counsel joined the conversation. The two of them crafted the remedy together and then "pulled [the defense counsel] in rather quickly." Defense counsel did not participate in crafting the remedy at all, other than to say, "Yes, Your Honor." In this, as in all things, the defense attorney is subordinate to the prosecutor and judge. When errors occur, defense attorneys don't notice them. When remedies are needed, it's not defense attorneys who propose them. Their only job is to say, "Yes, Your Honor."

Also, how can the defense attorney agree with the proposed remedy? Ten minutes prior to that conversation, he did not even know that there had been an error. Now, suddenly, he knows how to cure the error? Doesn't he need a few minutes to consider what damage this error may have caused and what cure is appropriate? Shouldn't he be allowed to check case law? Maybe a mistrial is required; he doesn't know. He is not competent or qualified to agree with remedies on his client's behalf.

The remedy to which this defense attorney so painstakingly agreed was the following: the alternates would henceforth be sequestered separately from the regular jurors, who would be told to start their deliberations over, as if that were possible.

A judge has nearly complete discretion to decide whether curative instructions will work or not. If he wants to use a curative instruction, he just tells the jury to ignore everything they just heard, and then the jury is magically presumed to do that. If he prefers a mistrial, he announces that he doesn't think a curative instruction would work. This he justifies with one of two hackneyed metaphors. The first, and more common, is, "You can't un-ring that bell." The second – less common, but more colorful – is, "You can't throw a skunk in the jury box and tell them it doesn't stink." Hackneyed cliches are invincible in the legal system; I've never seen one be challenged successfully.

In this trial, the judge decided that he could "un-ring the bell," so he gave the jurors the following instruction:

> Judge: To the rest of you, you are to continue. Start your deliberations over subject to the same instructions that I gave you, okay, how long it takes you to get back where you are now but to refocus yourself and start over.

With that instruction, I apologize for any inconvenience.

This instruction is ungrammatical and nothing about it is clear. First, the judge tells the jury to continue; then he tells them to start over. Then he qualifies his command with the following clause, "subject to the same instructions that I gave you." I assume they are supposed to ignore certain parts of the instructions, particularly the parts that pertained to alternate jurors, but it's not completely clear. He never instructs the jury to ignore everything the alternate had said to them. They are never instructed how, exactly, a jury goes about starting anew. Juries are laypeople. They have no legal training. I guess they're just supposed to know how to empty their minds of everything they had spent the previous day working on.

In the first go-round, the jury was instructed that the alternates were not to participate in any way. Well, they clearly did not follow that instruction. What makes us now believe that they will follow their new instructions? How many times must a jury ignore instructions before we can question the presumption that they always follow them? (The answer, my friend, is blowin' in the wind...)

Also, the note that the jurors wrote was filled with spelling errors and misused words: "accused" instead of "recused," "to hard" instead of "too hard," and "two sense" instead of "two cents." That's three errors in a note of only 26 words. Perhaps it is just my own intellectual snobbery, but is it wrong that these mistakes lead me to suspect that such a jury is unlikely to understand complicated instructions?

The jury spent half a day deliberating before receiving the curative instruction from the judge. After receiving it, they deliberated for only 25 more minutes before reaching a verdict. This casts serious doubt on the notion that they "refocused" themselves and started over. The verdict? Guilty.

This trial was for capital murder. So, after the guilty verdict, there was a second phase called the "mitigation" phase. While writing the jury instructions for this second phase, there was a brief but interesting exchange between the judge and the prosecutor.

Judge: Are they sequestered during the deliberations?

Prosecutor: I do believe so, yes. But this time I will double-check.

This exchange reveals the origin of the flawed instruction: the prosecutor wrote it. "But this time I will double-check," implies, "I should have double-checked last time." By the way, you almost never hear a defense attorney say that they will double-check a rule. Checking rules is not part of their job description. Their job, as they see it, is to let the prosecutor write the rules and to say, "No objection, Your Honor."

Notice also that the judge addressed his legal question to the prosecutor, not to defense counsel. The judge knows that defense counsel won't be participating in the writing of the mitigation phase jury instructions, so it didn't even occur to him to ask defense counsel; he knows they won't know the answer. This is not an isolated occurrence. It's quotidian and banal. Nobody is fighting for the interests of the defendant, which is fundamentally unfair.

After the guilty verdict, defense counsel submitted to the court a "Motion for a Mistrial," asserting that the alternate's presence and participation in deliberations rendered the jury verdict invalid. Already, defense counsel has blundered. A "Motion for a Mistrial" must be submitted before the jury reaches a verdict. After the verdict is reached, as was the case here, one must submit a "Motion for a New Trial," which is slightly different. It's a minor error. But these minor errors accumulate and accumulate until they become an avalanche of incompetence.

In the judge's ruling denying the Motion, he wrote:

> "First the court acknowledges that the decision to send the alternates back to the jury room was error. While others may have participated in and acquiesced to the decision, ultimately, the decision was the responsibility of the court."

Black's Law Dictionary defines the word "responsibility" as: "liable to be made either to suffer or pay compensation in certain eventualities." This judge is not going to make himself suffer or pay compensation in any way, shape, or form. Nowadays, powerful people, not just judges, but politicians, CEOs, billionaires, pretend that taking responsibility shows contrition, when really it's become a form of self-aggrandizement. It's more about advertising that the buck stops with them because of how powerful they are than it is about truly admitting fault and promising to do better in the future. "I take responsibility" is a show of contrition just as much as "I apologize for being so great and successful" or "I'm sorry that you took offense" is an apology.

So, while the judge claims to take responsibility, all he did was admit fault. And he didn't even really admit fault. It was other people's fault, but he's in charge, so he'll be a big man and take the blame. The remainder of his ruling is devoted to absolving himself of all responsibility:

"The error in this case, and the ground upon which defendant[40] relies in his motion for a new trial, was the court's instruction that allowed the alternate jurors to be present during deliberations.

"The jury instructions were prepared as a result of a great deal of effort, participation, and cooperation by both counsel for the state and the defendant. [They] met with the court and reviewed the initial draft of the instructions proposed by the state."

In legalese, when a trial takes place in state court, the prosecution is referred to as "the state." So, this excerpt from the judge's ruling is an admission that the flawed instructions were authored by the prosecution, not the defense. The judge tries to minimize the prosecutor's responsibility by writing that it was merely an "initial draft" that was merely "proposed" by the prosecutor, but the meaning is clear. The prosecutor was worried about "losing the alternate." When the time came to write the next set of jury instructions, the prosecutor said, "But this time I will double check."

As for the "great deal of effort, participation, and cooperation by both counsel for the state and the defendant," what really happened is that the state wrote the jury instructions in their entirety and defense counsel said, "no objection." Defense counsel didn't notice the flawed instruction. Perhaps he never read it. Perhaps he didn't know it was wrong.

"The defendant attempts to portray himself as a passive bystander – a passenger in a motor

---

[40] The motion was actually written by the lawyer, not the defendant, but courts refer to both as "the defendant."

vehicle on a road trip. Nothing could be further from the truth."

Lots of things could be further from the truth.

"The defendant never objected to the court's decisions. Rather, he specifically agreed with same."

True, but that's what a passive bystander does: never object. And what does a passenger in a motor vehicle do besides never object and specifically agree? A passenger goes along without touching the steering wheel. So defense counsel's portrayal in his "Motion for a Mistrial" is accurate.

"Finally, the record makes it clear that both the state and the defense were actively involved in crafting a solution to the problem."

False. The record makes clear that only the judge and the prosecutor crafted the solution. Defense counsel was "pulled in rather quickly" only after the solution had been crafted, and then said, "Yes, Your Honor."

"The defendant's active involvement in this case and the decision regarding the alternates is very important in deciding the motion for a new trial."

Now the motive for the exaggeration of defense counsel's involvement becomes clear. He is going to use it to justify his decision to deny the defendant a new trial.

"The waiver rule requires that a party make a contemporaneous objection to alleged trial error in order to preserve the error for appellate review. This rule is of long standing

130

and it goes to the heart of an adversary system of justice.

"[D]efendant's 'Motion for a New Trial' must be denied because he invited the error. A party will not be permitted to take advantage of an error which he himself invited or induced."

At this point, I must describe the doctrines of waiver, invited error, and plain error. All three are more germane to appeals than to trials; but in this case, they happened to come up during trial. So I will explain them now. The underlying concept is sensible. The courts can't let somebody cause an error, lose the trial, and then win on appeal because the trial was unfair due to the error that he himself caused. They also want to avoid situations where counsel knows that there has been an error that will win on appeal, so he keeps quiet about it and wants to see what the trial verdict will be. If the verdict is good, he never mentions the error. If the verdict is bad, he appeals, wins, and gets a new trial – sort of a "heads I win, tails I don't lose" situation. So those errors must be objected to at the time they occur, not later. Otherwise, those errors are waived, and you pretty much cannot appeal them.

But even rules with sensible origins can turn malignant and metastasize if they are not properly maintained. The present case is a perfect example. The judge used this rule to deny the defense attorney's motion for a mistrial, saying that he invited the error with the alternate jurors. But the defense attorney didn't invite the error. The prosecutor wrote the error into the jury instructions. The defense attorney allowed the error by failing to object when it happened. But this was due entirely to incompetence, not some clever ploy to get a new trial. Neither the judge nor the prosecutor noticed the error, either. Why are we expected to have a better understanding of the rules of court than either of them? The judge is well aware of this. He knows the prosecutor created the error. He uses the defense attorney as a scapegoat simply because he can.

When neither the lawyers nor the judge knows the law, the person who suffers is the defendant. He gets an unfair, error-filled trial. The U.S. Constitution guarantees the defendant a fair trial. But somehow, courts use the doctrines of waiver and invited error to trump the defendant's right to a fair trial. These doctrines are not in the U.S. Constitution, they are merely rules "of long standing," whatever that means. Why does a rule of long standing supersede a constitutional guarantee? The courts seem to be concerned only with the battle between the lawyers, making sure that neither lawyer gets an unfair edge, rather than ensuring that the trial is fair to both the defendant and the victim.

This is why defense attorneys' paucity of objections is so harmful to their clients. If a lawyer objects, the error can be reviewed on appeal. If a lawyer fails to object, the error must meet the "Plain Error" standard before it can be reviewed. The Plain Error standard is nearly insuperable. The appellant, to meet that standard, must prove, among other things, that but for that error, he would have won the trial. You can't prove a counterfactual. Nobody knows for certain what would have happened. So, for all intents and purposes, if your lawyer fails to object at trial, then you can't win on appeal.

Returning now to the judge's ruling, the judge will shift his focus from the failure of defense counsel to object to the conduct of the alternate jurors in the jury room.

> "The court in Murphy went on to hold, 'the party complaining of the error has the burden of showing that the alternates disobeyed the court's instructions by participating in the deliberations, either verbally or through body

language, or that their presence chilled the deliberative process.

"The record does not support a conclusion that the jury panel was complaining about alternate juror one. The defendant chose to edit the question to make it appear to support his position. The entire question reads, 'Can [Mr. C.] be accused from the jury because it's to hard for him to listen in without commenting or putting in his two sense.' The question indicated that it was hard for [Mr. C.], not that it was hard for the panel. Also, the question states that it was difficult for him to listen without commenting, not that he was indeed commenting.

"There is absolutely nothing in the record to support a conclusion that the alternate was participating in deliberations or was disruptive."

Absolutely nothing in the record?? The judge is blatantly lying. No reasonable person could read the jury's note and conclude that the alternate had not participated.

The panel called alternate one out by name. How could they call someone who was not participating out by name? He was sitting there perfectly quietly, but they could read his mind and knew he secretly wanted to participate? Remember, even gestures or body language constitute impermissible participation. Furthermore, the jury's note does not say that "It was difficult" for him to listen without commenting. It says that it was "too difficult," which means that he participated. He could not have not participated because it was too difficult for him to do so. The judge is twisting the juror's note to make it appear to support his position – precisely the sin he accused defense counsel of committing in their "Motion for a Mistrial."

Furthermore, the jury's note included the phrase, "or putting in his two sense," a phrase intended to belittle the alternate and express the jury's dislike of him and his comments. Recall than in an earlier note, the alternate had tried to have a regular juror kicked off the panel, which is the very definition of chilling[41] the deliberative process. How can the judge possibly believe the panel could use the expression "putting in his two sense" to describe somebody who was not participating? He cannot. He knows the jury's note was a response to the alternate's earlier note. The judge even said on the record, "As a way of background, I believe this question is a result of the last question from the jury."

The judge is lying, and his motive is obvious. He wants to avoid granting a new trial. He cites State v. Murphy in his ruling. Murphy derives from the U.S. Supreme Court case United States v. Olano (1993), where the justices wrote,

> "In theory, the presence of alternate jurors might prejudice a defendant in two different ways: either because alternates actually participated in deliberations, verbally or through body language; or because the alternates' presence exerted a chilling effect on the regular jurors."

Murphy and Olano say that an alternate must participate in deliberations for a new trial to be granted, so the judge will be as procrustean and dishonest as he needs to make the facts conform to his self-interest. If any of you reading this had any illusions that the criminal justice system

---

[41] Chill: v. To inhibit or discourage.

is a place where truth wins out over lies, that last excerpt from the judge's ruling ought to dispel those for you.

How often do judges lie and twist facts like this? As often as they need to. In case you were wondering, judges do not get penalized, punished, censured, or reproached in any way for lying. They have immunity. You can appeal a judge's ruling to a higher court and possibly get it overturned, but that's it. Some judges may find that mildly embarrassing. They might have to endure some ribbing at the office Christmas party: "Hey, Einstein! I heard you sent the alternates into the jury room! Real nice…"

This judge was very deliberate in his choice to cite Murphy rather than some other cases, but you can't know that solely by reading the text of his ruling. Murphy says, "the party complaining of the error has the burden of showing that the alternate disobeyed the court's instructions by participating in deliberations." Compare that to a different case, State v. Downour (2001):

> "If an alternate juror remains in the jury room
> during deliberations in violation of Criminal
> Rule 24 (G), the State has the burden of
> showing that this did not result in unfair
> prejudice to the defendant."

Downour puts the burden of proof on the prosecution. The judge chose Murphy because it placed the burden of proof on the defendant. This business with cherry-picking precedents in order to achieve predetermined outcomes has been going on for centuries. I quote now from "Gulliver's Travels," written over 300 years ago by Jonathan Swift:

> "It is a maxim among these lawyers that
> whatever hath been done before may legally
> be done again; and therefore they take special

135

care to record all the decisions formerly made against common justice and the reason of mankind. These, under the name of precedents, they produce as authorities to justify the most iniquitous opinions; and the judges never fail of directing accordingly."

Often, there are precedents for whatever the judge feels like doing. There could be nine rulings that say a mistrial is required and only one that says a curative instruction is sufficient. The judge will pick that one precedent that he likes. The other rulings will not be mentioned in his ruling. This form of judicial bias is more insidious because it is not found in what the judge said, but in what he did not say.

The judge concluded his ruling on the "Motion for a New Trial" with the following words:

"Finally, given the defendant's active participation, he cannot take advantage of an error he created. The defendant's motion for a new trial is OVERRULED."

So, when the judge, prosecutor, and defense attorney are all so incompetent that they make a mistake that violates the sanctity of the jury process and denies the defendant his constitutional right to a trial by an impartial jury: tough shit. Nine out of every ten appeals could be denied with those words: sure, mistakes were made, but tough shit.

Notice that the judge wrote that the defendant "created" the error because he "actively participated." All the defense lawyer ever said was "No objection, Your Honor." But even this seemingly innocuous bit of carelessness did great harm to the defendant because it blocked a chance to appeal. The defendant would have been better off if defense counsel had actually read the instructions and caught the error, because then the jury would have been impartial. The defendant would have been better off had counsel not read the instructions and not said "No objection," because then defendant could still have appealed. What the defendant actually got was counsel who did not read the instructions and said, "No objection." That is the worst of both worlds for the defendant.

The worst of both worlds for the defendant, obviously, is the best of both worlds for the prosecution. These actions, most likely, were the result of laziness and incompetence, but they are indistinguishable from collusion between prosecutor and defense counsel, because defense counsel did exactly what the prosecutor would want if they were colluding against the defendant. Many defendants, after they are found guilty, are left to wonder, "was my lawyer working for me or against me?"

In this chapter, we looked at one tiny decision by a judge during a trial: the decision to send the alternate jurors to the jury room. How many errors did this decision cause? Let us count.

> One: the judge, the prosecutor, and the defense counsel had an off-the-record sidebar, a violation.

> Two: the judge instructed the alternates to retire to the jury room but not participate in deliberations.

> Three and four: prosecutor and defense counsel agreed this was appropriate.

> Five: the judge summoned the alternate, told him again not to participate, and again sent him back into the jury room.

> Six and seven: prosecutor and defense counsel agreed this was appropriate.

Eight: defense counsel failed to object the following morning when judge and prosecutor proposed separating the alternates from the jurors and giving a curative instruction.

Nine: defense counsel submitted a "Motion for a Mistrial" instead of a "Motion for a New Trial."

Ten: the judge said defense counsel actively participated in writing the flawed instruction, a lie.

Eleven: the judge said defense counsel actively participated in crafting the remedy, a lie.

Twelve: the judge said there was "absolutely nothing in the record to support a conclusion that the alternate was participating in the deliberations or was disruptive," a lie.

A total of twelve errors: some were unintentional; some were intentionally designed to cover up the unintentional ones.

Twelve errors in one small part of one trial in one courtroom in one county in one state. This trial had many more errors than just the twelve presented here. There were errors during voir dire; there were errors in the handling of evidence; there were errors in the examination of witnesses; there were errors during the mitigation phase. Did the judge take responsibility for any of these? He said he did; but did he, really? The answer is no.

Consider what the Supreme Court wrote about the role of judges:

> "In a criminal prosecution, it is the judge, not counsel, who has the ultimate responsibility for the conduct of a fair and lawful trial; the judge is not a mere moderator, but is the

governor of the trial for the purpose of assuring its proper conduct and of determining questions of law."[42]

Does that sound like the judge in this trial? I don't think so. Now multiply all this by fifty states, by 50-100 counties per state, by up to 20 judges in a county, by however many trials take place in each courtroom. The result is a shitload[43] of errors.

17.2. Evidence: Circumstantial and Direct

Circumstantial evidence:

1. Evidence based on inference and not on personal knowledge or observation.

2. All evidence that is not given by eyewitness testimony.

Direct evidence:

Evidence that is based on personal knowledge or observation, and that, if true, proves a fact without inference or presumption.

DNA, fingerprints, footprints, etc., are all circumstantial evidence. Direct evidence is eyewitness testimony. The labels are confusing because "direct" sounds like it ought to be stronger than "circumstantial," when often the opposite is the case. DNA is generally considered stronger than a witness who was forty feet away, slightly drunk, in a space with poor lighting, etc.

---

[42] Lakeside v. Oregon (1978).
[43] Technical term.

If the evidence against you is mostly circumstantial, you will probably see the prosecution ask the following sorts of questions of potential jurors during voir dire: "How do you feel about circumstantial evidence? Do you feel you could weight it as heavily as you weigh direct evidence? Do you feel you could convict somebody based on circumstantial evidence alone?" Jurors who express hesitancy about circumstantial evidence will get challenged (removed) by the prosecutor.

17.3. Sidebars

When the judge was reading the instructions aloud to the jury, he was given pause by the flawed instruction to the alternates, so he summoned counsel to discuss it. This discussion is called a "sidebar." In a capital murder trial, it is required that all sidebars be recorded and on the record. Here is the rule in my state:

> Rule 22. Recording of Proceedings: In serious offense cases, all proceedings shall be recorded.

Capital murder is the most serious offense of all, so all proceedings definitely should have been recorded. This rule derives from the Sixth Amendment's guarantee of a "speedy and public" trial. When lawyers and judges have clandestine, off-the-record sidebars, that portion of the trial is not public, which is a violation of this guarantee.

But the judge didn't want this sidebar recorded because it might have proved embarrassing. If the instruction was correct, then the judge would look foolish for having questioned it. If the instruction was wrong, then the prosecutor who wrote it would look foolish. The trial transcript, at that point, reads simply, "Thereupon a sidebar was held outside the hearing of the court reporter and the jury."

As you can see, this is one of those rules that nobody really pays attention to and is almost never enforced – much like those speed limit signs on the highway that I mentioned in an earlier chapter. In this trial, the rule was violated with such indifference and nonchalance that it's clear that rules are violated all the time.

You might think that when trial courts blatantly violate rules, the defendant can get justice by appealing to a higher court. Nope. The appellate court will agree that the rule was broken, but you don't get a new trial, tough shit. Here is an example:

> "Trial court erred in failing to record sidebar conferences in a serious-offence case as required, but defendant, who failed to object and who accepted the trial court's summary of the sidebar conferences as accurate, was not prejudiced."[44]

It is unclear what the court would have ruled had Davis objected. Don't assume that if he had objected, he would have won. But it is clear that if you fail to object when it happens, you will not be able to win on appeal.

---

[44] State v. Davis (2014).

Chapter 18: Should You Take the Witness Stand?

Should you, the defendant, take the witness stand and testify in your own defense? After the choice between pleading guilty or going to trial, this is the most important decision the defendant must make.

Defendants have an absolute, constitutional right to testify on their own behalf. Defense attorneys can waive almost every right a defendant has without permission, but they can't waive this one. This is one of the few times that the judge talks directly to the defendant and asks him if he wishes to testify. Then the defendant, not his lawyer, must answer. The fact that courts have specifically protected this right suggests two things. One, it is a very important right. Two, many defense lawyers would waive their clients' right to testify if they could.

Most defendants choose not to testify. I really don't know what the percentage is but if I had to take a wild guess, I'd say 80 percent do not testify, 20 percent do.[45]

Most attorneys strongly advise most of their clients not to testify. Is that good advice? It's a very difficult question. Let's analyze it as best we can.

Typically, the defendant testifies last. Then the prosecution and defense make their closing arguments. Finally, the jury retires to deliberate. If the defendant testified, the jury will be given the following instruction: "You are to weight the testimony of a defendant by the same rules that apply to other witnesses." If the defendant did not

---

[45] It's difficult to find reliable statistics about trials. It would be nice to be able to look up the percentage of defendants that testify. Of those, what percentage win? Of those who do not testify, what percentage win? Why is it that I can easily look up Tom Brady's completion percentage on third down broken by home versus away game, but the percentage of defendants who testify and win is impossible to find?

testify, the instruction will be: "It is not necessary that the defendant take the witness stand in his/her own defense. He/she has a constitutional right not to testify. You must not consider the fact that he/she did not testify for any purpose."

This instruction tells the jury that they are not allowed to take your decision not to testify as evidence of your guilt. Juries are supposed to presume that you are innocent. Both are hogwash. Juries usually presume that the defendant is guilty. Juries also think that an innocent person would want to testify in order to defend himself, so any defendant who doesn't testify must be guilty. These are just two more of the fundamental, foundational presumptions of the justice system that everybody pretends are true even though, most of the time, they're not.

Know that when you make your decision. Your jury does presume that you are guilty, and, if you choose not to testify, they will consider that to be evidence of your guilt, regardless of what they were instructed.

Lots of defendants are guilty. They choose to go to trial because they feel the evidence against them is weak or wrong. They fear that if they testify, the prosecutor will outsmart them, trap them, trick them, and get them to incriminate themselves. Maybe so. Only you know your case. Only you know how skillfully you would be able to handle the prosecutor's questions. But based on the many transcripts I've read, the whole cat-and-mouse game between prosecutor and defendant is not a very big part of most actual cross-examinations. You see it all the time in TV shows and movies, but that's because it is very dramatic and exciting. It plays a smaller part in most real trials.

Even defendants who are 100 percent completely innocent are sometimes terrified of taking the stand. Partly this is due to fear of public speaking, fear of being made to stand up in front of the class and made to look like a fool.

Partly it is due to their fear of being tricked into saying things that make them appear guilty even though they are innocent.

Defense attorneys, in most cases, recommend that their clients not testify. In fact, sometimes, when a client insists on testifying, the lawyer will request (out of the hearing of the jury) to have it put in the record that the defendant is proceeding against counsel's advice.

Why is this? In a nutshell, your lawyer thinks that you are guilty, you are an idiot (at least as far as matters of law are concerned and probably in the rest of your life, too), that he is a genius (at least as far as matters of law are concerned and probably in the rest of his life, too), and he does not want your greasy, ignorant fingers contaminating the masterpiece he has assiduously created for your defense - a defense that, as we know, will consist entirely of asking the jury if they really, really, truly, truly believe that the prosecution proved their case beyond a reasonable doubt.

Why does your lawyer think that you are guilty? Because the police and the prosecutor told him that you are. He believes what they tell him, not what you tell him. Most of his clients are in fact guilty. But most of his clients plead guilty and don't go to trial. What portion of the clients that go to trial are guilty? That's another difficult question. He is not willing to think that hard. He thinks you're guilty.

Why does your lawyer think you're an idiot? First of all, maybe you are. You did get arrested, after all. Second, many of his clients are drug addicts, drop-outs, learning disabled, ADHD, schizophrenic, or bipolar. Third, you almost certainly don't know the law, especially the first time you get arrested. Nobody does, and this is by design. If people knew the law, they wouldn't need to hire lawyers. Having a bunch of laws that everybody knew and could easily understand would be bad for the lawyer business. This is paradoxical because the same people who write these abstruse laws then tell you that *ignorance of the law is no excuse*. But we're all ignorant of the law. Even judges and lawyers, especially defense lawyers, are frequently ignorant of the law, as has been demonstrated in several earlier chapters.

Why does your lawyer think that he's a genius? More than anything else, it is the nature of the job. He must present himself as an expert. That's why people hire lawyers: for their expertise. So if he doesn't act like an expert, no one will hire him. And all of the lawyers that he interacts with all day long are also acting like experts all the time. It's very disorienting and most lawyers can't resist getting swept up in this mass delusion of intellectual superiority.

Defense lawyers generally recommend that their clients not testify. If you have a criminal history, they will tell you that the prosecution is allowed to bring that up when they cross-examine you, whereas if you don't testify, it's off limits. Your lawyer will tell you that the jury won't believe your testimony if you have a criminal record, so by testifying you won't improve your chances and could do yourself harm. I don't know if this tends to be true or not, but I'm skeptical. Juries seem to have little difficulty believing all the criminals, reprobates, and scoundrels that testify against you. So if you were to take the stand and give a compelling account of your own innocence, I think most juries would be persuaded. It's hard to be certain. But I do know this: when the jury finds you guilty and the judge gives you the maximum sentence allowable by law, your lawyer will not apologize and say, "You know, you probably would have been better off if you had testified." No, he will remain convinced that you could only have made things worse even though the result you got by following his advice was the worst possible result.

Perhaps you and your lawyer have not decided whether or not you should testify by the time trial begins. No problem. You don't need to decide until everybody else's testimony is complete. If your lawyer asks potential jurors during voir dire how they feel about a defendant who doesn't testify, you'll know he doesn't want you to testify.

Finally, it's worth remembering that if you testify, it means a longer trial and more work for everyone: your lawyer, the prosecutor, the judge, the jury, everyone. It is in each of their interests that you not testify. It is uncanny how often the advice your lawyer gives you results in less work for him, not more.

My advice to you is this: you should expect a very weak defense by your lawyer in closing arguments. So, if you need a vigorous defense, you're going to have to do it yourself. If at all possible, you should testify. Of course, if you testify and lose, your lawyer will blame the loss on you. Whether you choose to testify or not, you will never be able to know what would have happened if you had made the opposite choice.

Chapter 19: Closing Arguments

The closing argument is the most important segment of any jury trial. While the things that prosecutors and defense attorneys say during closing arguments are not themselves evidence, this is the point in the trial where the attorneys summarize and explain all the evidence that was presented over the course of the trial in order to try to persuade the jury to find you guilty or not guilty.

The prosecutor gives his closing argument first because the burden of proof is on him. (Sometimes the prosecutor gets to go first and last; The defense's closing argument gets sandwiched in between.) He will be very clear and specific, telling the jury what the essential elements of each crime are and how the various pieces of evidence presented at trial fit together to prove each and every essential element beyond a reasonable doubt. The prosecutor will tell the jury with great certainty that they must return a guilty verdict because he has proved each element of each crime beyond a reasonable doubt.

When the prosecutor is done, the defense lawyer stands up and gives his side's closing argument. What he should do is two things. First, he should clearly and specifically describe to the jury all the evidence that proves you are innocent (e.g., the witness who said it wasn't you, the DNA sample that doesn't match you, the girlfriend who testified you were home all night with her, etc., etc.) Second, he should home in on the essential elements where the evidence is flimsiest and attack them mercilessly. These attacks should include clearly and unambiguously telling the jury that the prosecutor has failed to prove those essential elements; and because of that failure, the jury must return a not guilty verdict.

That's what the defense lawyer should do, but that's not what he will do. All the defense lawyer will actually do is make vague suggestions to the jury that maybe the evidence isn't quite as strong as the prosecution says it is. He will not say that the prosecutor failed to prove anything because that would make the prosecutor look bad and that might make him angry. Defense attorneys want to kiss the asses of prosecutors, not make them angry. When you read a lot of trial transcripts, you see over and over again that defense attorneys are obsequious and deferential towards prosecutors, not confrontational. Also, the defense attorney will never say that you are innocent, and he will not say that any piece of evidence proves that you are innocent, even if it does.

I don't expect you to take my word for such an important point as this. So, I will present two examples that demonstrate what I have asserted. The second example is taken from a capital murder trial. The first example is taken from a child sex case.[46] Please don't let this distract you. It is not my intention to condone or defend child molestation. But of all the trial transcripts that I have read, this is one of the clearest demonstrations of how defense attorneys desert their clients when their clients need them most.

In the first example, the defendant was convicted based on two pieces of evidence: the testimony of the child's mother, saying what the child had told her,[47] and the testimony of a nurse who examined the child for signs of bruises. I'll present excerpts of the prosecutor's and defense attorney's closing arguments pertaining to the nurse's testimony so that you can compare and contrast them. Then I'll present excerpts of the nurse's actual testimony.

---

[46] In prison, a person convicted of sex with a minor is called a "chomo," an appellation combining child-molester with homo. They're the lowest of the low in prison.

[47] You might think that such testimony would not be allowed because it is hearsay. But hearsay rules evaporate when the victim is a minor.

First, the prosecutor.

Prosecutor: "The nurse, in her results are uncontroverted injuries. You saw them. The nurse testified about them. They're there. They got there when the defendant used his fingers to penetrate. The testimony [of the mother] is backed up by the injuries. When you put them all together, there is proof beyond a reasonable doubt [of the rape].

That's all pretty clear, right? The testimony of the mother plus the injuries described by the nurse equal proof beyond a reasonable doubt of rape. It's safe to assume that every one of the jurors understood that argument.

Now let's look at the defense attorney.

Defense Lawyer: "And I listened to the testimony of the nurse. And the only comment I would like to make is that it's not as black and white as the state would lead you to believe with respect to her testimony about the injuries. Because her first impression - and she did not discount the possibility that she had caused the injury."

Far less clear and far less forthright than the prosecutor, he never says his client is innocent or that the prosecutor failed in any way to prove anything. The defense attorney suggested that the evidence was not quite as strong as the prosecutor said it was, but he never told the jury that there was not proof beyond a reasonable doubt - never. The prosecutor clearly said there was proof beyond a reasonable doubt, and the defense attorney never said there wasn't. So, what do you think the jury is going to decide? Proof beyond a reasonable doubt, of course. Now let's look at excerpts from the actual testimony of the nurse when she was on the witness stand.

> Nurse: "So initially I didn't think there was an injury, so I documented no injury with the initial exam. Then we did document after using the toluidine blue dye that... That location is a possible tear. So, you know, I wanted to, in all fairness, you know, when we didn't initially see it, we didn't want to assume that it was just there. We—you know, those are common areas that you could cause an injury with separation and traction, but so that's why I documented that."

OK, so what did the nurse say? First, she examined the child by eye and found that there was no injury and she documented that in her report. Then, later, she applied something called toluidine blue dye to the child's body and somehow that revealed "a possible tear:" not a "definite tear," a "possible tear." And then the nurse admitted that she, the nurse, may have caused the injury. When she says, "you could cause an injury with separation and traction," she is talking about injuries caused by the forceps she used when examining the child.

Let me be clear. What I have just presented is excerpts of the nurse's testimony, not the complete testimony. And I have deliberately selected those parts of the nurse's testimony that reveal the weakness of her testimony. But that is exactly what a defense attorney is supposed to do, home in on the weakest parts of the prosecution's case. A chain of logical reasoning is only as strong as its weakest link. So, a good defense attorney should identify the weakest links in the chain and attack there.

Now, I have no idea whether the defendant in this case is actually innocent or actually guilty. All I know is what

I read in the trial transcript. But I know that if the nurse wasn't sure there was any injury at all; and if there was, she's not sure that she didn't cause it herself during the examination, then that is not proof beyond a reasonable doubt that the defendant caused injuries.

Read the prosecutor's closing statement again. It is strong but inaccurate. He says the injuries are "uncontroverted." False. The nurse herself controverted them. She at first said there were no injuries and documented that in her written report. Then later she said there were injuries, thereby controverting herself. Now read the defense attorney's statement again. It is meek and ineffectual. The most he can muster is, "it's not as black and white as the state would lead you to believe." The difference in the forcefulness of those two closing statements was the difference in the trial. If the defense attorney had said that the prosecutor was lying and told the jury that the nurse's testimony left major doubts, then the defendant would probably have won.

Here is a second example, this one from a capital murder[48] trial.

> Defense lawyer: "Have they proven to you beyond a reasonable doubt that [the defendant] went to that house and killed [the victim]? And what about burglary? Did he go there and burglarize the home? The evidence in this case leads to a not guilty verdict."

Again, the defense attorney won't assert his client's innocence, won't attack the prosecution's evidence, and won't say that the prosecutor failed to prove a single thing.

---

[48] Capital-murder means the defendant can get the death penalty if the jury finds him guilty.

Asking the jury rhetorically whether they think the case was proved or not is not any defense at all. This kind of defense by non-defense is certain defeat for his client. Even though he never said so explicitly, every member of the jury can tell that he doesn't believe his client is innocent. If he had believed that his client was innocent, he would have said so. The jury knows that. So, they are going to find the defendant guilty, guaranteed.

If you think about it, the defense's strategy doesn't require any pretrial preparation at all. It doesn't even require going to law school. The lawyer just says "did they prove murder? Did they prove burglary? Did they prove rape? Really? Are you sure? Really?" Then he claps his hands together, collects his paycheck, and goes home. His defense is equivalent to rolling over and playing dead. Lawyers choose this strategy because it requires the least work. But it never wins. So, if you find yourself a defendant in this situation, beware.

It's important to point out, the defendant and the lawyer probably had meetings prior to trial where they discussed what the lawyer's strategy would be at trial. The lawyer surely told his client some version of, "I'm gonna hammer them on those bruises. They can't prove those bruises and without those bruises they have no proof at all that a rape took place." I promise you he did not say to his client, "Well, I'll just go in there and vaguely suggest that the evidence of the bruises is not super-duper strong." How can I promise that? Because no defendant would allow his attorney to do that to him. Any defendant in America would raise holy hell and start demanding a new lawyer if he had any inkling of just how weak a defense his lawyer was planning. So we can be quite sure the defense lawyer did a fair bit of lying to his client in any pre-trial or during-trial strategy meetings they had.

This is one of the reasons that lawyers don't want to have meetings with clients. At meetings, clients ask questions. And when clients ask questions, lawyers sometimes have to lie. Lying is an unavoidable part of the job for most lawyers. Solution? Minimize meetings with clients.

If you watch enough court TV, you will eventually see video from a courtroom where a lawyer sits down after closing arguments and the defendant launches himself across the table and punches his lawyer over and over as hard as he can until the bailiffs rush over and subdue him.[49] You also see this occasionally on the local 5:00 o'clock news. When this happens, the newsman will invariably say something to the effect of, "What an animal that guy was! We sure are lucky that he is going to prison," suggesting that nothing in particular ignited the defendant's violent outburst; it was just part of the defendant's savage nature. But even the most violent killers in the history of American criminal justice - even Ted Bundy, Sammy "the Bull" Gravano, Timothy McVeigh, and John Wayne Gacy wouldn't leap across a table in a crowded courtroom filled with armed guards to start pummeling their lawyer for no reason.

So you have to ask, what was the reason? More than likely, it was betrayal. What else could inspire that kind of violence? It was a bunch of phony promises of a vigorous defense followed by the roll-over-and-play-dead closing arguments like the ones presented in this chapter.

---

[49] Search "defendant attacks lawyer on YouTube and find many, many videos like this one, in which the defendant says to his defense lawyer, "You sold me out!" https://www.youtube.com/watch?v=dYX8jx6ZhzQ.

Chapter 20: Let's All Go to Prison

After receiving your sentence from the judge, you will be taken back to your jail cell. You'll tell the other inmates in the cell the news. They'll tell you to keep your head up and stay strong. Even the obnoxious and mean-spirited ones will be supportive. Maybe you'll make a few phone calls, tell family the bad news. Soon, you will roll up your mat, your books and papers, your snacks and hygiene products, and carry them all to a new cell where they keep all the inmates who are waiting to "ride out."

Now you are no longer presumed innocent. You are guilty and convicted. The difference is nominal. Everyone assumed you were guilty before trial and treated you as such, but now you officially are. Before, you would sometimes wonder how in the hell it was legal to treat an innocent person so abominably. Now that no longer matters to you.

In about a week, you will be awakened very early, given an orange jumpsuit, handcuffed, shackled, loaded on a bus and driven to the state's reception center prison. There you will be inspected, see-lected, dee-tected and nee-glected.[50] They do all this in order to determine your risk level and security classification so that they can decide which prison you will be sent to. Prisons are stratified by security level: minimum, medium, maximum, and supermax. (Leave it to the prison system to have something higher than maximum.[51] (Is there no definition they can't subvert, no oxy they can't moron?) Maximum security sometimes contains a wing for the state's death row inmates (only for states that still have the death penalty, of course).

Supermax is for inmates who have made multiple escape attempts, have killed another inmate while in prison,

---

[50] Arlo Guthrie, "Alice's Restaurant Massacree" (1967).
[51] Maximum: adj. 1. The highest amount, value, or degree attained or attainable. 2. n. An upper limit allowed by law or regulation.

or have beaten up a guard--that sort of thing. Medium security allows more time outside and more freedom of movement. Minimum has the most freedom of movement. If you behave yourself while you are in prison, they will eventually lower your security classification and send you to a lower security prison. If you behave badly, they will raise your security classification and send you to a higher security prison.

Everything is slow in prison. Everything takes longer than it seems like it ought to. It will take a month or two for the system to decide what your security classification should be.

If you went to trial, you will probably want to appeal your conviction and sentence. If, like most people, you pled guilty, you probably won't. In order to begin your appeal, you need to file a notice of appeal in the court that just sentenced you. You have about 30 days from the date of your sentencing to get this filed. If you miss that deadline, you'll need to file a motion for leave to file a delayed appeal. The word 'leave' here just means permission from the court. The court may grant you leave to file after the deadline, but they may not. So be safe and file your notice of appeal before the deadline. (Also, be aware that the rules and deadlines may be different in your state. You need to check all that in your state's "Rules of Court." All prison law libraries will have this book.)

Your trial lawyer, even if he is a total incompetent, should take care of this for you automatically. But you need to make sure he does, just in case. If your lawyer does not file your notice of appeal on your behalf, the court probably will not let you use his failure as an excuse. Get used to this. Everything the lawyers fail to do is your fault. The following is an interesting demonstration. In Ludwig v. United States (2000), the court wrote:

"However, with respect to counsel's failure to file a notice of appeal, every Court of Appeals that has addressed the issue has held that a lawyer's failure to appeal a judgment, in disregard of the defendant's request, is ineffective assistance of counsel regardless of whether the appeal would have been successful or not."

Right now, you're probably thinking I just lied to you. Clearly the court just ruled that the lawyer was at fault. Keep reading....

"We vacate the district court's order and remand this case for a determination of whether petitioner actually asked counsel to perfect[52] an appeal. Should the district court determine that the request was made but disregarded by counsel, so that petitioner was denied effective assistance of counsel, then petitioner will be entitled to a delayed appeal."

And then,

"On remand, the district court held an evidentiary hearing and concluded that Ludwig had not requested counsel to file an appeal. The court again denied Ludwig's motion to vacate."

Oooh, I'm so sorry. But we do have some lovely parting gifts for you. Thank you for playing, Mr. Ludwig.

Before your trial, the court didn't want to hear a peep out of you. They only wanted to deal with your lawyer. All

---

[52] 'Perfect' = complete.

messages from the judge or prosecutor were transmitted to you through him. All of your responses were transmitted back through him to the court and prosecutor. You were to be seen and not heard. Now suddenly, when that same lawyer fails you, you are supposed to know that A) you need to file a notice of appeal; B) you only have 30 days to file it; and C) you need proof that you asked your lawyer to file it for you. How would you know any of that?

Once the notice of appeal is filed, the court will instruct the stenographer to produce a hard copy of the transcript of your trial and sentencing. This usually takes between one and six months. Once the transcript is complete, the clock starts ticking on your appeal. The court will give you 45 days or so to write and submit your appeal, but you can ask for, and almost certainly receive, two 30-day extensions. If you have a court appointed appellate lawyer, he will definitely take these two extensions.[53]

Sometimes, the stenographer will send the transcript to your lawyer and then your lawyer will refuse to send a copy to you. He may say, "You are not entitled to a free copy. You must pay for it, a nickel a page." He may say, "It's not safe. One of the other inmates might steal it from you." These and any other excuses he might dream up are all bullshit. Do not accept his excuses and start the process of finding yourself a new lawyer. Once again, the courts will say that your failure to obtain your transcript is your fault and nobody else's. Here is a ruling that is so merciless that I can't help but laugh:[54]

> "Circumstances such as prison riots and lockdowns are not sufficient to establish good

---

[53] More on this in a later chapter.
[54] Ohio v. Lawson (2006).

cause for purposes of an application to reopen an appeal .... It is well established that difficulties securing both the transcript and assistance at a correctional institution are not sufficient to establish good cause."

The question remains as to whether global thermonuclear war would be sufficient to establish good cause, but prison riots and lockdowns are insufficient.

Chapter 21: Appeals

It's time for an overview of the appeal process, step by step, and the approximate amount of time each step may take.

21.1. Appeals Process Timeline

Step	Description	Time
1	File "Notice of Appeal"	1 month
2	Receive Trial Transcript from Court	4 months
3	Submit Direct Appeal Brief	4 months
4	Receive Prosecution's Reply Brief	2 months
5	Submit Your Response to Prosecutor's Brief	1 month
6	Receive Appellate Court Ruling on your Brief	5 months
6a	Win → Conviction Overturned, New Trial	
6b	Lose → Continue to State Supreme Court	
7	"Memorandum of Jurisdiction" State Supreme Court	3 months
8	Receive Denial from State Supreme Court	5 months
9	Write Habeas Corpus; Submit to Federal Court	12 months
10	Receive Prosecution's Reply Brief	2 months
11	Sur-reply to prosecution (a.k.a. "Traverse")	1 month
12	Receive Magistrate's Recommendation	8 months
13	Submit Objections to Magistrate's Recommendation	1 month
14	Receive Judge's Ruling on Habeas Corpus	6 months
14a	Win → Conviction Overturned, New Trial	
14b	Lose → Continue to Federal Court of Appeals	
15	Apply for Certificate of Appealability (COA)	2 months
16	Receive Denial of COA from Fed. Court of Appeals	3 months
17	Appeal to U.S. Supreme Court	2 months
18	U.S. Supreme Court Declines to Accept Case	5 months
END	**Approximate Total Time**	**67 months**

The whole process, from being sentenced in the Court of Common Pleas to being denied by the U.S. Supreme Court takes around 5 ½ years. About 26 months is spent writing and preparing briefs. About four months is spent waiting for the prosecution to write their responses in opposition to your briefs. About 36 months is spent waiting for rulings from the various courts. Your mileage may vary.

Every step must be done in order. You can't begin your appeal in federal court until you've exhausted your appeals in state court, meaning you must first write your direct appeal brief and then submit it to a state court of appeals (steps 3 - 6), and then file a "Memorandum of Jurisdiction" to the state Supreme Court (steps 7 - 8). So let's start at the beginning.

You file your "Notice of Appeal" and then wait around for the stenographer to produce the transcript of your trial. This takes approximately five months. You will probably spend the first two of those months at the state's Correctional Reception Center. The last three will be at whichever prison the state assigns you to after your security review and classification. This prison will be your "parent institution."

At your parent institution, there will be a law library where you can access reference books and computers to search case law. "Case law" just means rulings by other courts on other people's appeals. This will be an eye-opening experience for you. "What? You mean to tell me that alternate jurors are not allowed in the jury room? But in my trial, they...!" "Hey, the search warrant said first floor and second floor; it didn't say anything about searching the basement. How come my lawyer didn't object when they...?"

Once the transcript is ready, the clock starts ticking on your direct appeal. If you don't have money to hire a lawyer to write your appeal, the court is required to provide one for you. So you have four choices: 1) Hire a lawyer to write your appeal; 2) Have the court appoint a lawyer to write your appeal; 3) Do your appeal yourself;[55] 4) Don't appeal.

I should mention here that a couple of horizontal steps have been intentionally omitted from the list at the beginning of the chapter for the sake of simplicity. There is a parallel appeal you can make simultaneously with your direct appeal if you have brand new evidence that did not exist at trial, e.g., new DNA evidence, somebody else admits to the crime, an important witness recants their testimony, that sort of thing. I'm going to skip all that. All the advice I will give you about the direct appeal applies equally to these parallel appeals.

Once the direct appeal is complete (step six), the court is no longer required to provide lawyers, even for indigent appellants. From this point forward, you must pay for any lawyers yourself. Given that, if you have a limited amount of money, some people will advise you to let the court provide a lawyer for your direct appeal and save your money to hire lawyers for the later stages of the appeals process. This seems sensible, but it turns out to be bad advice.

What nobody tells you is that any time your lawyer makes a mistake, you can never get rid of it; you carry it with you forever. Like herpes. Everything your trial attorney fails to object to becomes res judicata[56] and procedurally barred. Res judicata just means "Too late. You missed your chance."[57] You can't appeal his failures in state court, and

_____

[55] When you do anything for yourself, i.e., without the help of a lawyer, it is called "pro se."

[56] Res judicata is Latin for "the thing has been decided."

[57] You actually can appeal his failed objections, but you have to meet the "plain error" standard, which is basically impossible. You can also try to get the appellate court to agree that your trial lawyer provided ineffective

you probably won't be able to appeal in federal court, either. Most states have a "contemporaneous objection" rule. In Wainwright v. Sykes (1977) the U.S. Supreme Court held that a petitioner who fails to comply with a state contemporaneous-objection rule is barred from habeas relief. (Just to be clear, they mean barred from habeas relief on that particular issue only, not barred altogether.) So your trial lawyer failed to object to some little lie the prosecutor told the jury? Four years later, when you receive the magistrate's ruling on your habeas corpus petition (step twelve), you'll see that the federal court has not forgotten this little "oopsie" that your lawyer made, and they continue to hold it against you.

Likewise, anything your appellate lawyer leaves out of your appeal brief becomes res judicata—dead; you are procedurally barred from ever raising that thing again.[58] So, if you allow the court to appoint a lawyer to you for your direct appeal, any lawyer that you hire to help you in later stages will be constrained by the decisions that the court-appointed lawyer made. If that court-appointed lawyer was an inept schmuck who failed to find any winning issues, the lawyers you hire later will only be allowed to raise those same losing issues. So you need to get the best lawyer you can afford at the earliest possible stage. Do not save your money for later stages.

Lawyers seem to be completely unaware that their decisions affect their clients, i.e., you, downstream. Each lawyer focusses entirely on his particular link in the

---

assistance of counsel, but for this you have to meet the "Strickland" standard which is also basically impossible. More on this in a later chapter.

[58] You can appeal for ineffective assistance of appellate counsel. This is another horizontal step I left out of the list at the beginning of the chapter. This appeal would occur between steps six and seven.

appellate chain and doesn't care at all about what comes later. Your trial lawyer doesn't care that his failures to object will handicap your appellate lawyer. Why should he? He is not an appellate lawyer, and when you finish your trial you get moved down the conveyor belt and he'll never see you again. Your appellate lawyer doesn't care that his failures will cripple your federal lawyer. Why should he? He's not a federal lawyer. He doesn't do habeas corpus. And when he finishes your appeal, you will be moved down the conveyor belt and he'll never see you again. I remind you that in your relationship with your lawyer, he doesn't see you as his client in the way that you understand the word 'client.' He sees you as the product. He does his job as quickly as possible, pushes the product down the conveyor belt, forgets about it entirely, and focusses on the next product arriving from the guy before him on the conveyor belt.

If you win your direct appeal, you get either a new trial or a new sentence. If you lose, you take your case to the state Supreme Court. You can't bring up any new arguments; you can only raise the same arguments you raised in your direct appeal.

What you write to the State Supreme Court is called a "Memorandum of Jurisdiction." It is different from an appeal. It is basically a sales pitch intended to persuade the Supreme Court to take an interest in your case. Rather than try to persuade the court that you are innocent or that you didn't get a fair trial, you must convince the Court that you are raising legal issues that are very important and of great interest to the general public of your state. If you can persuade them of that, they will accept jurisdiction of your case and you will then be allowed to appeal. If they decide not to accept jurisdiction, this simply means that they were not interested in the legal issues that you hoped to raise. They will send you a terse note from the clerk of the Supreme Court informing you that they have declined jurisdiction.

There will be no reason given and no comments on the merits of your case. You will learn nothing.

Don't be disappointed. Nobody ever gets the state Supreme Court to accept jurisdiction. I do not know anybody that had jurisdiction accepted; and I don't know anybody that knows anybody that had jurisdiction accepted. So, for all intents and purposes, it never happens. It's a mirage.

It takes about eight months, all told, to get your denial from the state Supreme Court (step eight). Given that you are guaranteed to lose, and you will receive no useful feedback from the court, why not just skip this step and go straight to Federal Court? Because the Federal Court will bar you from raising any issues that you did not raise in both your direct appeal and your Memorandum of Jurisdiction. So even though it is a complete waste of both your time and the court's time, you must go through this step.

The next step is habeas corpus in Federal court. "Habeas Corpus" is Latin for 'have the body." Forget about that. As far as we're concerned, habeas corpus just means "appeal in Federal Court." The main difference from your direct appeal in state court is that the Federal Court can only address violations of the U.S. Constitution. It cannot correct errors of state law that happened in your trial. This has to do with the separation of powers between state governments and the federal government delineated in the Constitution. Basically, states don't like the federal government telling them what to do, and a successful habeas corpus means a writ where the federal courts tell the state courts what to do.

Luckily, most errors of state law can be portrayed as violations of the Constitution most of the time. This is because the Fifth and Fourteenth Amendments promise you "due process of law." So you simply argue that when the state violated its own laws with the mistakes that it made at your trial, you did not get the "process" that you were due.

This trick can be pulled with most errors of state law, but not all. One conspicuous exception is rulings on the admissibility of evidence. The U.S. Supreme Court wrote: [59]

> "State court evidentiary rulings do not rise to the level of due process violations unless they offend... some principle of justice so rooted in the traditions and conscience of our people as to be ranked fundamental."

Translation: improper admission of evidence never ever rises to the level of due process violation. So don't bother bringing it up in your habeas corpus petition.

Now for some really bad news: you have almost no chance whatsoever to win your habeas corpus. It's another mirage. A study[60] published in 2012 found that of 2,384 cases being tracked, only fourteen resulted in the petitioner obtaining any relief, and of those 14, two were later reversed on appeal. (Don't forget that it's not just convicts who get to appeal. The prosecution also gets to appeal in those rare instances when they don't get a conviction, or the conviction is later overturned.)

$$14/2384 = 0.0059 = 1/170.$$

Pretty dismal. Then two were overturned dropping your chances to 1/199.

Petitioners win one out of 199. Be aware that "winning" in habeas corpus just means a new trial at which the petitioner will most likely be found guilty again.

---

[59] Estelle v. McGuire (1991).
[60] King, Nancy J. *Non-capital Habeas Corpus After Appellate Review: An Empirical Analysis* 24 Fed. Sent. Rep. 308 (2012).

The prosecution won two out of 14 appeals, which is 1/7. So their win rate is twenty-eight times better than the petitioners'. Does that look fair to you? It doesn't to me. Of course, I didn't read the actual petitions.

Are you familiar with the concepts of limits and infinite series from calculus? In calculus textbooks, you will see the following equation:

"$1/n = 0$ for large enough values of n." I use that same mathematical logic when I say that your chance of winning your habeas corpus is nil.

The U.S. Constitution "guarantees" you the "right" to habeas corpus:

> Article I Section 9: "The privilege of the Writ of Habeas Corpus shall not be suspended, unless when in cases of rebellion or invasion the public safety may require it."

Okay, it says "privilege," not "right," so at least they're being honest about that. But, last I checked, we are not being invaded. There is a little bit of rebellion going on, I have to admit. But come on, how is a zero percent chance of winning any different than a suspension of habeas corpus?

Habeas corpus has a peculiar two-step process. First, your petition goes to a magistrate. He makes a recommendation, not an actual ruling. You must file objections to these recommendations. If you don't object, the recommendations will become the official ruling and all those issues will thereafter be declared res judicata. If you do object, then an actual federal judge will look at your petition and rule on it. Ninety-nine percent of the time, the judge will simply follow the magistrate's recommendation. I'm not sure why they set up this two-step process. Just to reduce the workload of the bigwig judges, I assume.

After your habeas corpus, you appeal for a "Certificate of Appealability" to the federal court of appeals. They deny you. Then you appeal to the U.S. Supreme Court. They deny you. Then you're done. No more appeals.

The state Supreme Court is a mirage. Habeas corpus is a mirage. The U.S. Supreme Court is a mirage. This is yet another reason to spend any money you have getting the best direct-appeal lawyer you can afford. Once that first appeal is decided, you might as well spend your remaining money on lottery tickets.

Chapter 22: Habeas Corpus in State Court

There is a state court habeas corpus, too—at least, in my state. But it applies only to cases where the prisoner-petitioner has served his entire sentence, and the prison still refuses to let him out. Right now you're probably saying, "He served his whole sentence, and they still wouldn't let him out? I didn't know that could happen." Yup, it can happen. Check this out:[61]

> "Because Oliver has completed his maximum sentence, we hereby issue a writ of habeas corpus to Warden Eppinger, commanding Oliver's immediate release from incarceration."

The state Supreme Court issued that decision in June of 2018. Oliver should have been released in January of 2018, but the prison would not recognize that he'd served all his time and refused to release him. So, six extra months in prison. Yay!

I wonder what happens if you serve all your time, they refuse to let you out, so you climb the fence and make a run for it. Actually, I don't wonder—I know: they'll charge you with a felony escape attempt. But logically, once you've served your entire sentence, you're no longer being incarcerated; you're being kidnapped.

The prosecution filed a reply to Oliver's habeas petition opposing his release from prison. In the Supreme Court's ruling, they responded to each claim made by the prosecution. Here is one:

---

[61] State ex rel. Oliver v. Turner (2018).

> "Alternatively, Turner[62] contends that irrespective of whether Oliver's claim has merit, it is barred by res judicata...."

Recall from the previous chapter that "res judicata" means, "Too late. You missed your chance." So the prosecution is arguing that even if Oliver did serve his entire sentence, he should still have to serve more time that he was never sentenced to because he didn't ask to be released early enough. Huh? Only in a world where truth and justice mean nothing and res judicata and procedural violations mean everything could the prosecution make an argument like that. But that is exactly the kind of world the criminal-justice system is. And once you've inhabited that world for a long enough time, arguments like, "We know he served all his time, but we still want him to serve more," begin to make sense.

Also, we can assert, ipso facto, that the criminal justice system is a world where two people can look at a prison sentence handed down by a court of common pleas and disagree on what it means. This means, perforce, that A) either judges write sentences that are so unclear that even lawyers do not understand what they mean, or B) judges write clear sentences but some of the lawyers who read them are too stupid to comprehend their meanings, or C) all of the above. This is still another illustration of a point I made in an earlier chapter: The same lawyers and judges who write these abstruse laws then have the audacity to tell non-lawyers that ignorance of the law is no excuse. But we see that judges and lawyers are frequently ignorant of the law, and all their ignorance seems to get excused.

---

[62] In this particular case, the prosecution is called "Turner."

Chapter 23: Legal Research:
Where to Begin?

How do you do legal research? Where do you even begin? It's such a vast, deep, dark ocean. How do you dive in and how do you not drown? Many people are paralyzed with indecision. I'll teach you how to get started.

Your legal research begins at the prison law library. Find it. Go there. You will see inmates working there as law clerks. Some law clerks are competent; some are incompetent. Some law clerks are friendly and helpful; some are unfriendly and unhelpful. Obviously, you want to find the clerks that are both competent and helpful. When you reach the point where you can ask specific, not vague, questions, ask them. What you want to avoid are the clerks that are incompetent and friendly. They are the ones who will get you into trouble and lead you astray. When they don't know the answer to a legal question, instead of simply saying "I don't know," they bluff and lie. This probably began as a habit when they were in grade school and grew into a life strategy of using bullshit and false confidence to make it through. They dread being exposed as incompetent and ignorant.

Having just arrived at your parent institution, you probably have not yet received your trial transcript. There is very little you can actually achieve without it, but there is some. And since prison life is filled with free time, why not get started? (Is that a contradiction? Free time in prison?) The best place to start is with the documents you already have: the journal entry of your sentence and a copy of your indictment. You were given a written copy of your sentence (a.k.a. a "journal entry") a few days after the court sentenced you. This tells you what crimes you were convicted of, how much time you must serve in prison for each, and whether the time is to be served consecutively or concurrently.

Get the book called "Rules of Court" for your state. (If you're in a federal prison, get the "Federal Rules of

Court.") It's a big book, about the size of a phone book for a medium-sized city. It will have separate sections for civil rules, criminal rules, appellate rules, juvenile rules, etc., etc.... You start with the criminal rules. Scan the table of contents and find "indictment." Read all the rules that pertain to indictment. Here is an example of what you might find:

> "Crim R. 7(B) The indictment shall be signed in accordance with Crim R. 6(C) and 6(F)."

So, you flip back to Crim R. 6(C) and 6(F).

> "Crim R. 6(C) The foreperson shall administer oaths and affirmations and shall sign all indictments."

> "Crim R. 6(F) An indictment may be found only upon the concurrence of seven or more grand jurors. When so found, the foreperson or deputy foreperson shall sign the document."

Now you look carefully at your indictment. Was it signed? By whom? Was it the foreperson? What if it was signed but the signature is completely illegible? How do I know it was the foreperson who signed it?

How do I find out how many grand jurors concurred with the indictment? I don't know. I'll ask the law clerk on duty and see if he knows. Is he one of the good clerks? I'll ask around and see if I can figure out who the good ones are.

Now you go back and finish reading Criminal Rule 7(B):

> "Crim R. 7(B) Each count of the indictment shall state the numerical designation of the statute the defendant is alleged to have violated. Error in the numerical designation

or omission of the numerical designation shall not be grounds for dismissal of the indictment, or for reversal of a conviction, if the error or omission did not prejudicially mislead the defendant."

This rule seems self-nullifying. It says they *shall* state the numerical designation of the statute, but if they don't, nothing happens. No penalty. You can't use that to overturn your conviction.

Well, at least they're up-front about it. Normally, you find a rule that they've clearly violated, and you get excited thinking you're going to win on this issue and it's not until three hours of slogging through case law that you learn that courts won't do anything for that particular rule violation.

Next, you look up each numerical designation in the indictment. These are not found in the criminal rules, they are found in the state "Criminal Law Handbook." So you go up to the desk and return the "Rules of Court" and ask for a copy of the "Criminal Law Handbook."

Let's say that one of the crimes you were charged with is 2911.211 Aggravated Trespass. The handbook says:

2911.21 Aggravated Trespass

"(A)(1) No person shall enter or remain on the land or premises of another with purpose to commit on that land or those premises a misdemeanor, the elements of which involve causing physical harm to another person or causing another person to believe that the offender will cause physical harm to that person."

You read that and you think to yourself, "Hey wait a minute. I didn't cause harm to anybody, and I never intended

180

to cause harm to anybody.... Also, what misdemeanor was I charged with?"

If your eyes became glassy while reading that statute, you probably didn't notice how vague and ambiguous it was. If you were at a friend's house and got into an argument and he decides at any point that he feels threatened by you, regardless of whether you are actually threatening him, then the instant he formed that opinion, even if he didn't tell you, you were committing aggravated trespass because you were now remaining on his premises and you caused him to believe that you would cause physical harm to him. Also, must the misdemeanor specify in its elements that the person believes that you will cause them physical harm or not? The placement of the word "or" in the statute makes this unclear.

So now you need to get on the computer and search for cases where somebody appealed a charge of Aggravated Trespass on the ground that he had no intention to commit physical harm to another person. You sit down at the computer and click on the icon that says "Lexis Nexis."

The front page for Lexis Nexis appears. You need to understand the interfaces for the various databases. I'm not going to go into detail on this. Just try to follow along with my example and be aware that your version of Lexis Nexis may be very different. Click on the link for "Cases from the State Court of Appeals." Then find the box that lets you search by exact phrase. Type in "aggravated trespass," hit "search," and a list of several hundred cases pops up. Click on the top one. Up comes, for example, State v. Applegate, 2014.

Now you need to know how to read a case. Cases all have the same layout, the same structure. This allows you to scan them very quickly and see if they contain information that is useful to you. Cases are laid out as follows:

1. Case Name and Citation
2. Case Summary
3. Outcome
4. Headnotes
5. Opinion
    a. Procedural History
    b. Facts of the Case
6. Analysis
7. Judgment
8. Dissenting Opinions, if any

Near the top will be a case summary telling you what the major legal issues were, followed by the outcome. Generally speaking, since you are in prison, that means you lost your trial and therefore you prefer to find cases where the appellant won his appeal. Such cases usually say "Outcome: Judgment Reversed and Case Remanded." Where the appellant lost his appeal, it will say "Outcome: Judgment Affirmed."

Every once in a while, you come across cases where it is the prosecution, not the defendant, who appeals. That means the defendant won at trial and the prosecution is not happy about it. In those cases, it is the defendant who wants "Outcome: Judgment Affirmed" and the prosecution who wants "Judgment Reversed."

Next, you come to a section called "Headnotes." Most of the time, this is the only section you need. The headnotes are an outline of all the important legal issues in the case. So scan the headnotes and see if the legal issue you are interested in is there. If it is, you click on that headnote and it takes you right to the paragraph in the case where that issue is discussed. If it's not, close that case and move on to the next one.

Next comes the opinion rendered by the court. This will begin with the procedural history of the case: the date of the trial, the outcome of the trial, any previous motions or appeals made in the case, that sort of thing. Then come that facts of the case, e.g., "On January 12, defendant Applegate entered the Springfield Youth Recreation Center..."

Next comes the analysis by the appellate court. This analysis usually starts with a quick restatement of the "Assignments of Error" that the appellant raised in his appeal brief. For example:

> "Assignment of Error One: The Trial Court's Finding of Guilt for the Offenses of Aggravated Menacing and Aggravated Trespass are in Contradiction to the Manifest Weight of the Evidence."

The court will then summarize the argument that the defendant-appellant made in his appeal:

> "Appellant argues his conviction for Aggravated Menacing and Aggravated Trespassing is against the manifest weight of the evidence because the record indicates that until Potts, the store trainee, threatened appellant, neither Potts nor the other employees were in fear of appellant and appellant's behavior was not threatening. Appellant also asserts the employees did not order him to leave, but rather, asked him to remain and shop."

Okay, this looks promising. The appellant, Applegate, disputes that his behavior met the legal definition of Aggravated Trespass, same as we are trying to do.

A couple of words of warning here. These recapitulations by courts of appellants' arguments are opportunities for courts to recast arguments into something easier to deny (more later on how they do this). Also, the appellant, in his "Assignment of Error," combined two errors into one. He combined "the store employees did not feel threatened" with "the store employees did not ask him to leave." The appellant naturally believes that the court must refute both prongs of his assignment of error. But courts often pick the easier of the two, refute it, and ignore the more difficult prong altogether. To avoid this problem, create a stand-alone assignment of error for each assertion that you want the court to address.

Next comes the court's analysis and decision.

> "At the outset, we note that appellant correctly asserts that certain facts set forth and relied upon by the trial court in finding him guilty of both offenses differ from the testimony at trial. Nonetheless, we find that appellant's conviction for aggravated menacing and aggravated trespassing is not against the manifest weight of the evidence."

So, he lost on this issue. Appellant argued that his conviction was against the manifest weight of the evidence; the court ruled that his conviction was not against the manifest weight of the evidence.

Next comes a more detailed analysis and explanation of why the appellate court reached the decision that it did. These more detailed analyses usually take one or two pages and include citations and references to the precedents the court is relying on to justify its decision. On the computer, these references are hyperlinks that are lit up in blue. You can just click on them, and you will immediately pull up that case. Nice! In the bad old days, you had to go back into the library shelves and find the volume of the court record that contained the case you want. Nowadays, just click and it pops right up. Some aspects of modern technology definitely make life better.

Here is an excerpt from the court's analysis.

> "In conducting its review, the appellate court reviews the entire record, weighs the evidence and all reasonable inferences, considers the credibility of witnesses, and determines whether in resolving conflicts in the evidence, the court clearly lost its way and created such a manifest miscarriage of justice that the conviction must be reversed and a new trial ordered. The discretionary power to grant a new trial should be exercised only in exceptional cases where the evidence weighs heavily against the conviction."

We already know the outcome: the court denied there was error and the appellant lost. Let me point out one troublesome phrase: *"The discretionary power to grant a new trial should be exercised only in exceptional cases."* Once a court makes a statement like that, every other appellate court can cite that as a precedent and deny your appeal simply by asserting, with no proof, that your case is not "exceptional." What is an exceptional case? Who knows.

In one appeal that I wrote, the court used these sorts of phrases eight times to deny my claims.

> "Thus, after an independent review of the record, the court does not deem this to be so extraordinary a case as to relieve petitioner of his procedural default."

> "Antiterrorism and Effective Death Penalty Act of 1996 (AEDPA) ... imposes a highly deferential standard for evaluating state court rulings and demands that state court

decisions be given the benefit of the doubt. Petitioner cannot meet these high standards here."

"In light of this very deferential standard, the undersigned finds that petitioner cannot show that habeas relief is warranted."

And so on. Courts use these phrases as magical incantations to deny appeals whenever they have no other way to get the job done. These denials are entirely irrefutable:

Court: You don't meet the high standard. Denied.

Appellant: Why not?

Court: Because the standard is so high.

Appellant: Yes, I know it's high. I knew it was high when I submitted my appeal. I think my appeal meets the high standard.

Court: It doesn't.

Appellant: Why not?

Court: Because your appeal wasn't high enough.

Appellant: Okay. How high was it?

Court: Not high enough.

Appellant: You already said that.

Denials of this sort contain no information. They are logically equivalent to just saying "no." All an appellant can really say in response is, "Yes, my appeal does meet this very high standard that exists entirely in your head."

What is the point, really, of specifying that a remedy should "remain rare?" If three appeals all meet the manifest miscarriage of justice standard, the court should deny two of them to make sure that the remedy remains rare? Are we grading on a curve now? If there is a manifest miscarriage of justice, the appellant should be granted a remedy. It should not matter what happened in other peoples' appeals.

So, Applegate tried to appeal on an issue similar to yours and he lost. On the bright side, at least you're now doing legal research! You're reading criminal rules and procedures. You're reading definitions of crimes from the criminal law handbook. You're searching for helpful cases on the computer. That's 80 percent of what legal research is.

Now that you're done with the Applegate case, you continue down the list and see if you can find cases that closely resemble yours. See if you can find some where the appellant won. When you find a good case, click on the button that says "Shepardize." This will pull up a list of every other case that cited the good case that you just found. See if some of them won their appeals. See how similar they are to your case. You learn a lot by doing legal research. As I said in the previous chapter, it is an eye-opening experience. This is because your legal research didn't begin until after you lost your trial. You probably didn't do any legal research prior to trial. If you were in county jail, you couldn't get access to any legal materials. If you were out on bond, you probably did not go to a law library to find books on criminal rules and procedures. You probably don't even know where the nearest law library is. Your lawyer did not encourage you to do research; he wanted you to relax and leave everything to him. But now that you're in prison and you witnessed just how pusillanimous and ineffectual he was at trial, you realize how naive you were to have gone along with that.

Once your transcript arrives, you repeat the method you just learned over and over and over: find a rule or definition you think they violated, find the portions of your transcript that demonstrate these violations, search the Lexis Nexis database for case law where the appellant raised the same issues as you, and see how the courts ruled. Easy-Peasy.

Chapter 24: Ineffective Assistance of Counsel

The most commonly raised error on appeal, by far, is ineffective assistance of counsel. I would like to say that this is proof that most defense lawyers are ineffective, but I cannot. The main reason it is so common is that it is not specific to any particular crime. Appeals of conspiracy convictions tend to raise errors pertaining to the difficulty of proving conspiracy. Appeals of drug trafficking convictions tend to raise issues of illegal search and seizure. Appeals of rape convictions tend to challenge DNA evidence, the right to confront the witnesses against you, that sort of thing. But ineffective assistance of counsel is universal and can be raised in every appeal.[63] It is this universality that puts ineffective assistance at the top of the most-raised errors list.

The right to effective assistance derives from the Sixth Amendment, which says, *"In all criminal prosecutions, the accused shall ... have the Assistance of Counsel for his defense."* The Supreme Court said that the right to assistance of counsel means the right to effective assistance of counsel. It is not enough to have a warm body sitting silently beside the accused, the lawyer must provide effective assistance.[64]

In order to understand how courts evaluate claims of ineffective assistance, we have to look at two U.S. Supreme Court cases, both from 1984: Strickland v. Washington[65] and United States v. Cronic.[66] In these two rulings, the Supreme Court established the tests and standards used to distinguish

---

[63] Unless you represented yourself at trial. This is known as acting "pro se." If you were pro se, then you can't claim ineffective assistance of counsel.

[64] McMann v. Richardson 397 U.S. 759 (1970).

[65] Strickland v. Washinton 466 U.S. 668 (1984).

[66] United States v. Cronic 466 U.S. 648 (1984).

constitutionally prohibited ineffective assistance of counsel from constitutionally permissible assistance of counsel.

The more important of the two is Strickland v. Washington. In Strickland, the defendant, Washington, confessed to three counts of first-degree murder, multiple counts of robbery and kidnapping, assault, attempted murder and conspiracy to commit murder. The judge said he had tremendous respect for defendants who take responsibility for their crimes and admit what they have done. Then he sentenced Washington to death.

Washington appealed his death sentence and claimed that his counsel had been ineffective because he had failed to:

1) move for a continuance to prepare for sentencing,
2) request a psychiatric report,
3) investigate and present character witnesses,
4) seek a presentence investigation report,
5) present meaningful arguments to the sentencing judge,
6) investigate the medical examiner's reports, and
7) cross-examine the medical experts.

Washington lost his appeal and his death sentence was affirmed. The Supreme Court ruled that counsel's performance could not be deemed unreasonable, and, even if it was, Washington was not prejudiced by it. Nevertheless, this is the ruling where the Supreme Court established what has come to be known as the "Strickland Standard," the two-pronged test to determine whether a lawyer's assistance has been so deficient that it requires reversal of a guilty verdict.

The test is:

1) You must show that counsel's performance was deficient. This requires showing that he made errors

so serious that he was not functioning as the counsel guaranteed by the Sixth Amendment.

2) You must show that the deficient performance by counsel "prejudiced" the defense. Prejudice here means that, "but for counsel's unprofessional errors, the result of the proceeding would have been different." Essentially, you must prove that if counsel had not made those errors, you would have won your trial.

Three gigantic problems with this test leap out at me. First problem: it is perfectly acceptable for a defense lawyer to give his client terrible assistance, so long as it cannot be proven that the terrible assistance caused the outcome of the trial to change from not-guilty to guilty. The Supreme Court said so explicitly:

> "An error by counsel, even if professionally unreasonable, does not warrant setting aside the judgment of a criminal proceeding if the error had no effect on the judgment."

So counsel can give you incompetent assistance all day long with no penalty whatsoever, so long as you cannot prove that his incompetent assistance is what cost you the trial. Here is more:

> "Judicial scrutiny of counsel's performance must be highly deferential. A fair assessment of attorney performance requires that every effort be made to eliminate the distorting effects of hindsight, to reconstruct the circumstances of counsel's challenged conduct from counsel's perspective at the time. Because of the difficulties inherent in making the evaluation, a court must indulge a strong presumption that counsel's

performance falls within the wide range of reasonable professional assistance; that is, the defendant must overcome the presumption that, under the circumstances, the challenged action might be considered sound trial strategy."

They bend over backward to protect defense counsel from scrutiny. That paragraph is replete with adjectives and adverbs whose only purpose is to prevent criticism of defense attorneys: "highly deferential," "every effort," "strong presumption," and "wide range." They seem extremely concerned with the difficulties inherent in evaluating incompetent representation and not the least bit concerned with the difficulties inherent in proving that the lousy lawyer was responsible for losing the trial.

This ruling means that appellate judges have defense lawyers' backs. It is not necessary to posit some secret conspiracy here. It's all in writing if you read the case law. Phrases like "highly deferential" are problematic because courts use them to deny appeals without any other justification: "Sorry, we've got to be highly deferential. You lose."

Also, when it is simpler to prove that the error did not change the outcome of the trial, courts are not obligated to examine counsel's ineffectiveness at all. The Supreme Court wrote:

> "A court need not determine whether criminal defense counsel's performance was deficient before examining the prejudice suffered by the defendant as a result of the alleged deficiencies; if it is easier to dispose of an ineffectiveness claim on the ground of lack of sufficient prejudice, that course should be followed, so that ineffectiveness

claims do not become so burdensome to defense counsel that the entire criminal justice system suffers as a result."

That last clause is baffling. Ineffectiveness claims are not burdensome to defense attorneys at all. So what did the Supreme Court mean?

Also, wouldn't a criminal defendant like to know about all the bad mistakes that the lawyer he is about to hire has made, not just the ones that were proven to have cost his clients the trial? The number of errors that can be proven to have changed the outcome of the trial is a small fraction of the total number of errors made.

In baseball, they record every error that a fielder makes. They then use that information to decide who makes the all-star team, who gets a gold glove, who gets the highest salary, etc. They don't say, "Well, Rodriguez clearly made an error there but, since the Yankees ended up winning the game anyway, we're not going to bother to record it." So why do courts only care about errors that changed the outcome of the trial? The courts work very hard to protect the egos of defense attorneys and sweep as much evidence of their incompetence as possible under the rug.

You might say, "Hold on a sec. I'm sure appellate courts do this to make their own jobs easier. They don't want to waste their valuable time analyzing errors only to then determine that the error can be ignored because it was not outcome-determinative." Maybe, but that's not what the Supreme Court wrote. They said quite specifically that they don't want ineffective assistance claims to become burdensome to defense counsel.

So what incentive is there for defense counsel to work hard and give effective assistance? I ask you, dear reader, isn't the criminal justice system founded on the notion that if you want to change somebody's behavior from bad to good, then you must punish them when they do bad? Why doesn't the justice system apply the same principle when dealing with defense lawyers? Is it because they want to protect their own? Is it because prosecutors actually prefer that defense attorneys remain incompetent?

Second problem: it is impossible to prove what would have happened had the defense attorney not made the error he made. It is impossible to know what a jury would have done if defense counsel had been competent. As the Supreme Court wrote:

> "Of all the rights that an accused has, the right to be represented by counsel is by far the most pervasive for it affects his ability to assert any other rights he may have."

Ineffective counsel is like cancer. It spreads throughout the entire trial. But appellate courts say that it is not sufficient to prove that the deceased had cancer, you must also be able to identify the specific cancerous cell that caused the death. It's practically impossible. But courts do not care. Meanwhile, they care an awful lot—one might say they are obsessive—about "the distorting effects of hindsight" when criticizing a defense attorney.

Third problem: the definitions used by the Supreme Court in explaining the Strickland standard are circular. How do you decide if counsel's assistance was ineffective? The Supreme Court wrote:

> "This requires showing that counsel made errors so serious that counsel was not functioning as the counsel guaranteed the defendant by the Sixth Amendment."

That definition has the word 'counsel' on both sides of it. If I were to express that requirement mathematically it would look like this:

Prove counsel $\neq$ counsel

It is useless.

This is not just any old dumbass court in some Podunk backwater. This is the Supreme Court of the United States of America. When I read these rulings, I sometimes start to question my sanity. Maybe it's my fault, I tell myself. There is simply no way that the nine best lawyers in the United States could all sit down together and write such abject claptrap. I must be missing something. It simply cannot be that I'm right and the nine smartest lawyers are all wrong.

That is why I am so grateful for the existence of dissenting opinions and most especially for the opinions of Justice Thurgood Marshall. He lets me know that I am not completely nutso. Behold:

> "My objection to the performance standard adopted by the Court is that it is so malleable that, in practice, it will either have no grip at all or will yield excessive variation in the manner in which the Sixth Amendment is interpreted and applied by different courts. To tell lawyers and lower courts that counsel for a criminal defendant must behave "reasonably" and must act like "a reasonably competent attorney" is to tell them almost nothing.... In my view, the Court has thereby not only abdicated its own responsibility to interpret the Constitution, but also impaired the ability of the lower courts to exercise theirs."

Right on, Thurgood! That standard is wack!

Here is another nice paragraph from Marshall:

"[i]t is often very difficult to tell whether a defendant convicted after a trial in which he was ineffectively represented would have fared better if his lawyer had been competent. Seemingly impregnable cases can sometimes be dismantled by good defense counsel. On the basis of a cold record, it may be impossible for a reviewing court to confidently ascertain how the government's evidence and arguments would have stood up against rebuttal and cross-examination by a shrewd, well-prepared lawyer. The difficulties of estimating prejudice after the fact are exacerbated by the possibility that evidence of injury to the defendant may be missing from the record precisely because of the incompetence of defense counsel. In view of all these impediments to a fair evaluation of the probability that the outcome of a trial was affected by ineffectiveness of counsel, it seems to me senseless to impose on a defendant whose lawyer has been shown to have been incompetent the burden of demonstrating prejudice."

These things that Justice Marshall has written are obviously true. That means that not only are they true, they are also obvious. So how is it possible that eight ostensibly intelligent people, who all went to the most prestigious universities and law schools, served for years as federal judges, and then were hand-picked by presidents of the United States and interviewed and confirmed by the Senate, could all decide to impose a "senseless" burden on appellants? They know full well that it is unfair. If they weren't sharp enough to figure it out on their own, Justice Marshall told them so explicitly. And yet they chose to impose it anyway. Who benefits from this? Does it benefit justice or fairness? No. Does it benefit American society as a whole? Who the hell knows? I don't know and they don't know either. Nobody knows. Does it benefit defense attorneys? Yes. It protects them from criticism and conceals their incompetence. Does it benefit prosecutors? Yes. It makes it easier for them to get convictions because the defense counsel who oppose them are allowed to be ineffective. Does it benefit trial judges? Yes. They have to spend less time retrying cases overturned due to ineffective assistance. Does it benefit appellate judges? Yes. They need to spend less time analyzing ineffectiveness. This is all yet another example of the point I have made several times already: the court system was built by lawyers for lawyers.

One last quote from Justice Marshall's dissent:

> "To afford attorneys more latitude by 'strongly presuming' that their behavior will fall within the zone of reasonableness is covertly to legitimate convictions and sentences obtained on the basis of incompetent conduct by defense counsel."

Justice Marshall is right on point yet again. The Supreme Court knows that defendants are often convicted as a result of incompetent defense, and they are fine with it.

Interestingly, in 1994, Justice Blackmun wrote about the impotence of the Strickland standard in a dissenting opinion[67] to McFarland v. Scott:

> "[t]en years after the articulation of that standard, practical experience establishes that the Strickland test, in application, has failed to protect a defendant's right to be represented by something more than a person who happens to be a lawyer."

The Strickland test is unfair to appellants. The U.S. Supreme Court, along with anybody else that has bothered to look, knows this. And yet, even though it was written more than 40 years ago, nobody has bothered to try to fix it. And over those 40 years, defense attorneys have gotten less and less and less effective. How does that old saying go, "Spare the rod, spoil the child?" Well, we have been spoiling both defense attorneys and prosecutors for a long, long time now.

Strickland v. Washington focused on factors intrinsic[68] to the trial, i.e., it addressed specific errors made at trial by defense counsel. There is a second important case, also from 1984, for evaluating claims of ineffective assistance of counsel: United States v. Cronic, which focused on claims based on extrinsic[69] factors.

---

[67] As an aside, dissenting opinions are almost always better written and more interesting to read than majority opinions. I think this is because majority opinions must be acceptable to multiple justices whereas dissenting opinions are usually just one justice writing for him- or herself alone, everybody else's opinions be damned. This leads to more compelling writing and less dilution of opinions.

[68] Intrinsic: adj. Belonging to a thing by its very nature.

[69] Extrinsic: adj 1. Not essential or inherent; 2. being, operating or coming from without.

In 1980, Cronic was tried for mail fraud. Just before trial began, his retained counsel withdrew. So the trial judge appointed a lawyer to represent Mr. Cronic. He gave him a real estate lawyer who had never handled a criminal case and had never taken a case to trial before. They gave the new lawyer 25 days to prepare for trial even though the government had spent 4 ½ years preparing its case against Cronic, and there were boxes full of documents requiring review. At trial, Cronic was convicted on 11 out of 13 counts of mail fraud and sentenced to 25 years in prison. Cronic appealed his conviction in 1982 and won. He argued that there was simply no way that an inexperienced lawyer could have provided effective assistance in such a complicated case under those conditions.

But the U.S. government appealed Cronic's appellate court victory to the U.S. Supreme Court, which reversed and remanded (meaning that the government won and Cronic lost), holding that the criteria used by the Court of Appeals did not prove that counsel's defense had been ineffective. The Court ruled that Counsel's preparation time, his inexperience, and the complexity of the case did not justify a presumption of ineffectiveness, writing:

> "This conclusion is not undermined by the fact that respondent's lawyer was young, that his primary practice was in real estate, or that this was his first trial. Every experienced criminal defense attorney once tried his first criminal case."

Cronic got sent back to the appellate court and told to submit a new appeal with new ineffectiveness claims, that this time alleged specific errors made by trial counsel. He won that.

The appellate court remanded to the trial court for a new trial. The trial judge showed extreme hostility towards

Cronic. For example, at a hearing to reinstate Cronic's bond, Cronic at one point said, "Thank you," to which the judge responded, "Well, you're not welcome. I think you're a swindler and a cheat and you wouldn't see the light of day if I had my choice."

Later, when it came time to appoint new counsel to assist Cronic with his trial defense, this same judge appointed a brand new federal public defender and gave him only nine days to prepare. The public defender filed a motion for additional time and the prosecution did not object, but the judge denied the motion anyway. This was less time than Cronic's previous attorney had been given to prepare for the first trial.

Cronic lost his second trial—surprise, surprise. So he appealed yet again and won. The Federal Appellate Court wrote in its ruling:

> "Harrison P. Cronic appeals his conviction on 11 counts of mail fraud based on charges arising out of a check kiting scheme. Although couched in terms of sufficiency of the evidence, Cronic's main contention on appeal is, essentially, that an unembellished check kiting scheme is not a crime under that portion of the mail fraud statute which criminalizes schemes to obtain money by means of false or fraudulent pretenses, representations or promises. In view of Williams v. United States (1982), we reluctantly agree. Because the jury instructions limited the jury's consideration of evidence to that portion of the statute, and because the government failed to prove any false pretense, representation or promise, we are obliged to reverse Cronic's conviction."

And that's it. Cronic got out. He had been arrested in 1980 for purported crimes that took place in 1975. He finally won his appeal and was released in 1990. He served ten years in prison for something that turned out to be *"not a crime under that portion of the mail fraud statute."* One has to suspect that if he'd had competent counsel in the first place, he would have been found not guilty at his first trial, given that, as it turns out, he had not actually committed a crime.

None of the judges seemed to have had the slightest remorse about those ten years he served in prison for those non-crimes. Rather, the Court of Appeals said that they were "reluctant" to admit that he had not committed a crime, and the trial judge said he did not deserve to "see the light of day." Cronic sure seemed to make an impression on people. His first lawyer left him, and every judge seemed to loathe him. Maybe he had poor hygiene or chewed his food with his mouth open or something like that.

Going back to Cronic's Supreme Court case in 1984, it was here that the criteria were established for assessing claims of ineffective assistance of counsel based upon extrinsic factors. These factors include:

1) The time afforded for investigation and preparation,
2) The experience of counsel,
3) The gravity of the charge,
4) The complexity of possible defenses, and
5) The accessibility of witnesses to counsel.

But remember, Cronic failed to prove ineffectiveness extrinsically. The Supreme Court overturned his win in the appellate court, and he went back and proved ineffectiveness intrinsically.

So, even Cronic was not able to meet the Cronic standard. Recall that Washington was not able to meet the

Strickland v. Washington standard. His death sentence was upheld by the Supreme Court, and he was put to death two months after. So, even the two legal standards for ineffectiveness of counsel were not reachable by the people for whom they were named. It's a bit like finding out that Pythagoras never actually figured out the length of the hypotenuse of a right triangle, but they went ahead and named the theorem after him anyway.

If you've read this far, it won't surprise you to hear that people almost never win their claims of ineffective assistance. An analysis of approximately 4,000 federal- and state-reported appellate decisions regarding claims of ineffective assistance of counsel between 1970 and 1983 found that only 3.9 percent resulted in a finding of ineffective counsel.[70] Notice that the study stopped before Strickland and Cronic went into effect. The success rate of ineffectiveness claims is far lower now.[71]

I don't want to give you the impression that ineffectiveness claims never, ever win. Let's look at a few that did.

In Sanders v. Ratelle (1994), the Ninth Circuit Court of Appeals granted an ineffectiveness of counsel claim where a murder defendant's attorney failed to interview another person who had confessed to the killing. This potential witness had not only confessed to the crime on several occasions in a consistent manner, but he voluntarily went to counsel's office to tell him what actually happened, and counsel refused to see him. Then this same witness

---

[70] Burkhoff & Hudson *Ineffective Assistance of Counsel* (1993).

[71] Klein, Richard *The Emperor Gideon Has no Clothes: The Empty Promise of the Constitutional Right to Effective Assistance of Counsel* (1986).

showed up for trial, possibly to testify, and counsel told him to leave.

So, if your counsel makes certain that you get convicted even though you are innocent and another person has confessed to the crime, you may have a chance to win your ineffectiveness claim. Ineffective is a misnomer here. Ratelle's counsel was extremely effective—at getting him convicted. What possible justification could there be for shooing away a witness who admits to the crime, thereby exonerating your client? I can only think of one: you want your client to lose. Maybe the lawyer had a personal grudge against this client. Maybe the lawyer had agreed to lose the case in exchange for something from the prosecutor. Who knows?

In Javor v. United States (1984) the court granted ineffective assistance of counsel to an appellant whose counsel had been unconscious or sleeping during a substantial portion of the trial. You may chuckle at that, but contrast it with United States v. Katz (1970), where defense counsel, "on two occasions was observed to be sleeping while [the prosecutor] was examining a witness," and the court ruled that this was not ineffective assistance, writing, "…but this conduct did not require the trial judge to set aside conviction unless it prevented Katz from receiving a fair trial."

In summary, you have less than a one percent chance to win your ineffective assistance of counsel claim. The game is deliberately stacked against the defendant/appellant and in favor of the incompetent attorney. The courts know what they are doing. They protect the attorney at all costs.

Chapter 25: Dirty Tricks

Appellate judges[72] have a toolbox full of dirty tricks that they can use whenever they feel like denying an appeal. Most of these are just modernized, legalistic versions of the sophistries and logical fallacies that dishonest debaters have been using since the time of the ancient Greek philosophers.

25.1. Ad Hominem

One of the most common is a version of the ad hominem argument in which courts ignore the contents of the appellant's argument and focus instead on the fact that he was found guilty at trial. This trick is particularly galling because usually, the appellant is trying to prove that his trial was unfair. So, the appellate courts use the result of the unfair trial to prove that the trial was fair. The argument goes something like this:

> Appellant: My trial was unfair due to errors A, B, and C.
>
> Court: You were found guilty at trial. Therefore, A, B, and C are harmless. Appeal denied.

I have, several times, tried really hard to fight with courts over this one. For example, in one motion for summary judgment[73] that I wrote, in which I accused the prosecutor and the defense attorney of fraud and collusion at

---

[72] It would be more accurate to say "law clerks." You may think that judges do their own research and then write the opinions themselves. Most don't. They let their law clerks write their opinions. Then they give the law clerk's writing a quick going-over and put their name on it as if they wrote it. (See "*The Little Book of Plagiarism*" by Posner).

[73] Summary judgment is what you ask for when the opposing side does not oppose your argument.

trial, neither one offered any counter evidence—they just ignored my claim—so I moved for summary judgment.

The rules for summary judgment are:

> Federal Rules of Civil Procedure 56(a)
>
> The court shall grant summary judgment if the movant[74] shows that there is no genuine dispute as to any material fact and the movant is entitled to judgment as a matter of law.

Because the opposition neither denied my assertions nor offered any evidence to contradict me, I wrote in my motion that there was no genuine dispute as to any material fact and that the movant was entitled to a new trial due to prosecutorial and defense misconduct. The federal judge denied the motion for summary judgment with some specious procedural arguments and then concluded with the following sentence, "Further, the record indicates substantial evidence of guilt."

> So, I appealed, writing:
>
> "Petitioner's guilt or innocence is irrelevant to the granting of summary judgment. The rules for summary judgment do not say that only innocent people may be granted summary judgment. By explicitly basing his ruling on petitioner's guilt, the judge violates petitioner's Fourteenth Amendment right to equal protection under the law. The law is supposed to protect the innocent and the guilty alike."

---

[74] Movant = the guy initiating the motion. (Me in this case).

I lost.

25.2. New Flaws

Another dirty trick that appellate courts like to use is to raise some new flaw in an appellant's argument that was never raised by the prosecution. It goes like this: Appellant argues that the trial was unfair for reasons A and B. The prosecution then submits their reply, rebutting A and B. Next, the appellant submits his response to the prosecution's reply, in which he challenges the state's rebuttals to A and B. Now all the arguments are in. The appellate court must rule and decide between the appellant and the prosecution. Who made the more persuasive case? The appellate court denies the appeal for reasons P and Q, totally new reasons that the prosecution never raised; and because the prosecution never raised them, the appellant never had a chance to even foresee any need to rebut them or defend against them.

An appellant cannot defend himself against every counter argument that the prosecution raises in addition to every counter argument that the appellate court *might possibly* raise in the future. He can't anticipate every possible objection to his argument, and even if he could, these appeals and replies have page limits. There is not enough space to raise and refute every possible objection.

25.3. The Ever-Changing Kaleidoscope of Weak Evidence

This leads to a third dirty trick that I call "The Ever-Changing Kaleidoscope of Weak Evidence." It works like this: at trial, the prosecution shows the jury multiple pieces of evidence that vaguely suggest guilt. The defense attorney puts up no real defense. He never objects, he never contradicts, and he never says that his client is innocent. So, the jury finds the defendant guilty.

On appeal, the defendant-appellant tries to prove that there was no real evidence against him and that the defense attorney was ineffective for failing to make his case to the jury. He focuses on one of the weakest pieces of evidence. Let's call it evidence A. Appellant argues that A was illegally obtained by the police and does not prove that he is guilty anyway.

The appellate court will rule as follows:

> "Even if this court accepts that A was illegally obtained and that it was not indicative of guilt, this error is harmless because the jury had evidence B, C, D, E, and F, which were more than sufficient to allow the jury to return a guilty verdict. Since the error is harmless, the question of whether it was illegally obtained is moot, and furthermore, appellant cannot show that his trial counsel was ineffective because he cannot show that he was prejudiced[75] by counsel's failure to challenge evidence A. We therefor deny…"

Then, when defendant challenges evidence B, the appellate court will say, "Yes, but the jury could still have returned a guilty verdict based upon A, C, D, E, and F." And so on for C, D, E, and F. This is the "Ever-changing Kaleidoscope of Weak Evidence."

Speaking of page limits, there is a rule in federal Habeas Corpus proceedings that an appellant may have some

---

[75] Prejudice: it changed the outcome of the case from a win to a loss.

procedural violations excused if he can show that his state did not provide an adequate remedy for him to raise his issue. Well, I had a situation in which there had been so many serious errors made at trial that I simply could not fit them all into my 60-page appeal. So I asked the court to grant me a 15-page extension. The court decided that it would grant me only a 5-page extension. No reason was given for this decision, but this of course meant that there were some issues that I had to leave out of my appeal for lack of space.

So when I got to the Habeas Corpus phase, I thought, "Gee, I had issues that I was unable to raise in state court because I wasn't granted the full extension that I had asked for. Another way of saying that would be that the state remedy available to me for addressing the errors made at trial (direct appeal) was inadequate to my needs. This led to a farcical back-and-forth with the Federal Court.

First, I argued that my procedural defaults should be excused due to inadequate page limits. The court responded:

> "Petitioner[76] argues that [the state's] page limitations on appellate briefs establishes cause for his failure to raise claims on direct appeal; however, the record[77] does not support his argument. Petitioner filed a 65-page brief. Nothing prevented him from presenting additional claims in his appeal."

Umm... yes, something prevented me from presenting additional claims: the page limit. Obviously, if I ask for permission to write a 75-page brief and you allow me

---

[76] Petitioner = me.

[77] The record: the official report of the proceedings in a case, including the filed papers, a verbatim transcript of the trial hearing, and tangible exhibits. Also termed (in some jurisdictions) the clerk's record.

only 65 pages, and then I fill up all 65 pages to the very last line of the page, it should be quite clear that I would have written more if I had been allowed the space to do so.

So this "nothing prevented him from presenting additional claims" is a lie; but not just a lie, it's a complete 180-degree reversal of the truth. The court deliberately prevented me, and then when I complained, they said nothing prevented me. These are the kind of lies that Vladimir Putin tells. "Yeah we both know it's a lie, but I have nuclear weapons, so what are you gonna do about it, little man? Nothing? Then sit down and shut up."

Also, they included this little gem: "However, the record does not support his argument." They're saying that the record does not support my argument that I was forced to leave stuff out of the record. I would have been willing to let this argument go until they wrote that.

Instead, I fought back, writing:

"Also, how can the record show evidence of what was left out of the record? Was petitioner supposed to include a list of all of the errors he would have liked to have raised but could not at the end of his appellate brief? The magistrate's requirement that the record show evidence of claims the petitioner could not raise is logically insurmountable and unfair. It is simply not possible to show evidence of that which was left out."

I didn't win, of course. The Federal judge wrote the following in his denial:

"[Petitioner] also claimed that he did not raise many of those claims because the state appellate court limited the length of his brief. The district court rejected the argument because the record did not show that he could not have raised those claims."

And then they simply said that they agreed with the district court.[78]

25.4. *Repetition*

This is an example of a dirty trick I call "repetition." The lower court makes a bad ruling. I appeal. In my appeal I include all the reasons why the lower court's ruling was bad. Then the higher court simply restates the lower court's ruling verbatim and writes, "We agree with the lower court," ignoring every reason I adduced explaining why the lower court was wrong. Using this trick, they can easily sidestep all of the appellant's arguments.

Sometimes, they never explicitly state that they agree with the lower court. They restate the lower court's ruling and sort of imply that they agree with it without saying so. It's almost as if they don't want the dishonest and self-serving words of the lower court ruling to sully their ruling.

Sometimes, instead of repeating verbatim a lower court ruling, the courts will lift sections out of the prosecution's opposition brief and present them, unchallenged and unedited, as justifications for their denials. Sometimes it seemed to me as if the prosecutor was writing the denial of my appeal instead of the judge. It was if they had a tacit work-sharing agreement: the judge lets the prosecution win the case; in exchange, the prosecutor has to do all the work of researching case law and writing the decision for the judge. It works out great for the judge: less

---

[78] I appealed to the U.S. Supreme Court, but they just decline to accept jurisdiction without giving any reason - so that's the end of the line.

work. It works out great for the prosecutor: he wins all his cases. It works out horribly for the defendant/appellant: he is playing a rigged game and cannot win. But remember, he is just the "product" in the legal system, so who cares?

This was always my suspicion, of course, but I could never prove it. Well, I still can't prove it, but I've found some evidence that I am not the only person who feels this way. I read a book called "False Justice" by Jim Petro, the former attorney general of the state of Ohio. In it, he wrote:

> "The state of Ohio answered our motion and requested summary judgment (outright dismissal) in writing, claiming that our motion offered nothing new. On May 28, 2008, our team replied, countering the state's position. We waited with some confidence for the judge's decision.

> "Five weeks later, on July 9, 2008, Judge A. J. Wagner ruled. It was almost as if we were reading the prosecution's brief again. The court overruled our motion for post-conviction relief and sustained the prosecution's motion for summary judgment. We lost across the board."

I direct reader's attention to the phrase, "It was almost as if we were reading the prosecution's brief again." All I can say to that is, perhaps you were, Mr. Petro. Perhaps you were.[79]

---

[79] In the legislature, it is well known, although rarely mentioned, that congresspeople do not actually write the laws that regulate industries. Lobbyists write the laws. Banking lobbyists write banking regulations. Railroad lobbyists write railroad regulations. Oil lobbyists write environmental regulations. This phenomenon is known as "regulatory

25.5. Magic Words

Another dirty trick that I would like to point out is one I call "magic words." Magic words are like trump cards that allow the courts to win their arguments whenever they want to. In the page limits argument above, the magic words that the court used were, "the record does not reflect..." A court can put those five words in front of anything and then declare themselves the winner.

Let's say I spend many hours poring over an 800-page trial transcript and all the police reports show that the defendant left the bar long before the fight started and therefore could not be guilty of assault. I fill my appeal with quotes from the transcript and excerpts from the police report.

The court simply writes "The record does not support the claim that the defendant could not have committed the assault." No quotes. No excerpts.

The court's claim implies, of course, that they actually read the entire record. But they don't have time to read 800-page transcripts. So they simply recite the magic words "the record does not reflect..." and then they automatically win.

Sometimes the magic words come from the Rules of Court. For example, the rule for a challenge to the sufficiency of the evidence states that the court must

---

capture." It allows politicians to spend their time fundraising rather than understanding difficult regulatory problems. I do not see why the same phenomenon could not manifest in criminal courts. Call it "Judicial Decision Capture" and replace lobbyists with prosecutors. Other than that, there is no difference.

"perform a *de novo*[80] review of the record" and then find that "no rational trier of fact"[81] could believe that the evidence was sufficient.

So the court simply writes, "After a *de novo* review of the record, the court finds that no rational trier of fact would dispute that the evidence was sufficient to sustain a guilty verdict." Did they actually review the entire record de novo? Of course not. Do they actually have some test for determining what a rational trier of fact could believe? Nope. They just recite the appropriate magic words and then they get the outcome they want.

The Rules of Court has become like a book of magic spells. It does not prescribe procedures and actions that courts must perform; it is, rather, a list of specific words that courts must say. As we all know, it is far easier to say things than to do things, and since there is nobody who is going to tell the court that they are lying, this has become the way the courts work.

25.6. Straw Man

Another dirty trick used by prosecutors and judges is the straw man.[82] This one goes back to at least ancient Greek times. It goes like this: Appellant makes a strong argument. The prosecution, in their opposition brief, restates the appellant's argument in their own words, being sure to change the meaning in a way that weakens it. The appellant, in his reply brief, argues "Hey, wait! They have recast my argument. They didn't actually address the issues that I

---

[80] De novo = new.
[81] Rational trier of fact? I'd like to meet that fucking guy.
[82] Straw man: a weak or imaginary argument that is set up to be easily defeated.

raised." Then when the judge makes his ruling, he simply accepts the prosecution's straw man version of the argument, ignores the appellant's protestations that his argument has been unfairly recast, and then denies the appeal.

One particularly common form of the straw man arises when the appellant has a piece of evidence that proves his innocence. For example, let's say there is a video of the defendant in another town at the exact time that the crime took place, or the DNA excludes him as a possible contributor, or some other powerful proof of evidence. The prosecution will recast the appellant's argument from, "the evidence proves my innocence," to "appellant argues that the evidence does not prove his guilt beyond a reasonable doubt," which is obviously weaker than proof of innocence.

The appellate judge will then rule as follows: "Appellant argues that there is insufficient evidence to prove his guilt. We disagree. There is more than enough evidence for a jury to find defendant guilty, including…," and now will come a laundry list of weak evidence: DNA evidence at the crime scene was "consistent" with appellant's DNA; a witness said she saw a man of about appellant's height running from the crime scene; appellant's ex-girlfriend said that although he never actually hit her, she sometimes feared that he would. Appeal denied.

In a world where defendants were actually presumed innocent, there would be no real difference between "I can prove I'm innocent" and "You can't prove I'm guilty," and this particular straw man would not be so pernicious. But in the real world where defendants are usually presumed guilty, and appellants are always presumed guilty, this straw man is a crusher. It is ironic that prosecutors have actually found a way to use the presumption of innocence *against* defendants and appellants.

25.7. The Road to Nowhere

Another nasty trick that judges and prosecutors use is something I call "The Road to Nowhere." In an earlier chapter, I joked about the cruelty of the court's ruling that it is "well established" that prison riots and lockdowns are not sufficient to establish good cause to excuse a procedural default such as missing a filing deadline. How, exactly, could such a thing become well-established?

How many times in the history of the criminal appellate system has an inmate argued that the reason their appeal was late was that a prison riot prevented them from filing it on time? Prison riots don't happen every day. What does "well-established" mean exactly, anyway? It sounds as though there was a prison riot many, many years ago; an inmate was late with his appeal, and he tried to use the riot as an excuse. The court then did a thorough analysis from which it concluded that the prison riot did not excuse the late filing. Then it happened again in another prison—there was another riot, another missed deadline, another thorough analysis resulting in the conclusion that the riot did not excuse the lateness. And this happened again and again until it became "well-established" that you simply cannot use a prison riot to excuse a missed deadline.

How many times would such a thing have to have happened before it became well-established? Two? Ten? One hundred? What if you want to challenge something that is well-established? Does well-established mean it is irreversible until the end of time? Forever is a mighty long time.

In mathematics, it was well established for hundreds of years that nobody could prove Fermat's last theorem; then somebody proved it. For millennia, it was well established that human beings could not fly; then the Wright brothers did it. A mere 65 years later, human beings were flying back and forth to the moon.

Before it became well-established, what reasoning did the courts use to establish it? What rationale did the court provide in its denial of that very first inmate?

I went back to the case in question, Ohio v. Larson, 2006. Larson cites an earlier case, Ohio v. Quinnie, 2000, that said, "Prison riots, lockdowns, and other library limitations" are repeatedly rejected as constituting "good cause" for untimely filing. So we've progressed from "well established" to "repeatedly rejected," still with no actual logic or evidence that an appellant could challenge.

Quinnie cites Ohio v. Oden 1996, which says the following:

> "On March 7, 1994, appellant filed an application for reopening pursuant to Appellate Rule 26(B), alleging as good cause for failure to file within 90 days… that he was pursuing various appeals and collateral attacks on the judgment and that riots at the Southern Ohio Correctional Institute also impeded his ability to file a timely application. The court of appeals denied the application, finding that appellant failed to file the application in a timely manner, rejecting the stated reasons for good cause."

Here is the upshot: thirty years ago, there was this guy named Oden. He missed a deadline that he had 90 days to meet. He cited, among his several excuses, that there had been a riot at his prison which "*also* impeded" his filing. The court did not accept Oden's excuse, and, within two citations, Quinnie and then Larson, it had become "well established" that prison riots may never excuse a missed filing deadline.

This all seems absurd until you realize that laws are written by lawyers for lawyers. Lawyers do not care about prison riots or anything else that happens in prison because lawyers are not in prison. If Oden or Quinnie or Larson had hired a lawyer, then the prison riot would not have made them miss their deadlines. Serves those guys right for not spending their money on a lawyer. That's the bottom line.

25.8. Beyond a Reasonable Doubt

Finally, I want to take a close look at the "beyond a reasonable doubt standard" because dirty tricks abound here, too. One frequently hears lawyers say that, "beyond a reasonable doubt" is the highest standard of proof in the American legal system, but once you get to the court of appeals, you find out just how false that statement is. Courts have many standards that are much higher than beyond a reasonable doubt. They accomplish this in two ways: by explicitly using a higher standard or by applying preconditions to the reasonable doubt standard.

25.8.1 Explicit

I wrote earlier that Habeas Corpus is a mirage. Nobody wins their Habeas appeals. Here is the law, as it is applied in federal court, for a prisoner trying to get his conviction overturned because the state court judge did not follow the law:

> "The appropriate measure of whether a state
> court decision unreasonably applied clearly
> established federal law is whether the state

adjudication was objectively unreasonable and not merely erroneous or incorrect.

"It bears repeating that even a strong case for relief does not mean the state court's contrary conclusion was unreasonable. To obtain Habeas Corpus relief from a federal court, a state prisoner must show that the state court's claim being presented in federal court is so lacking in justification that there was an error well understood and comprehended in existing law beyond any possibility for fair-minded disagreement."[83]

Note that last line: "beyond any possibility." That is far higher than "beyond a reasonable doubt." Far higher.

25.8.2 Preconditions

There is a second, sneakier way that courts achieve standards of proof far stricter than "beyond a reasonable doubt." Here is an example.

When people are found guilty based upon very little evidence, they often try to appeal by claiming that the evidence upon which they were convicted was insufficient to sustain a verdict of guilt beyond a reasonable doubt. Here is the test that appellate courts use when evaluating these claims:

"the test for sufficiency of the evidence is whether, after viewing the evidence in a light most favorable to the prosecution, any rational trier of fact could have found the

---

[83] Harrington v. Richter (2011).

essential elements of the crime proven beyond a reasonable doubt."

Notice that the test has the words "beyond a reasonable doubt" right in it. But it also requires the court to look at the evidence "in a light most favorable to the prosecution." Obviously, this makes the reasonable doubt bar much, much higher, practically insurmountable. It's like telling a runner that he must jump over a high hurdle, *and* that he is only allowed to hop on one leg. The hurdle hasn't gotten any higher, but the constraint that courts have applied about how you are allowed to approach it has made it insurmountable.

When courts apply constraints and preconditions to the reasonable doubt standard, the result is a standard much stricter than reasonable doubt. This is obvious, really. If the constraints and preconditions didn't make the standard tougher, the courts would not have gone through the trouble of adding them.

This has been a fairly thorough sample of dirty tricks used by appellate courts. Courts use many other types of sophistry[84] and casuistry[85] as well. So be on the lookout.

---

[84] Sophistry: n. A subtle, tricky, superficially plausible, but generally fallacious method of reasoning.
[85] Casuistry: n. Oversubtle, fallacious, or dishonest reasoning.

Chapter 26: The Death Penalty

People love to debate the death penalty. Does it deter crime? Does it safeguard society? Is it cruel and unusual? Is it moral? How about for juveniles? Is it moral to execute juveniles? Is it racist? Does it discriminate against the poor? They tell us stories about heinous crimes committed by irredeemable murderers who don't deserve to live. They tell us stories about wrongly convicted men who are exonerated after serving 15 years on death row, or worse, after being executed.

All of this debate is interesting in an academic sort of way, but really doesn't make any difference. Here is how decisions actually get made: people watch the evening news on television. They see a report about a murder. There is a reporter with furrowed eyebrows and deep concern in his voice carrying a big microphone. Behind him are flashing red sirens and bright yellow police tape. Sometimes there are neighbors or grieving family members to interview. The viewer sees the report and then thinks either, "The guy who did that ought to die," or, "I don't think he ought to die for that."

This decision comes entirely from the gut. They don't give any thought at all to whether it makes their community safer or anything else. If the crime makes them feel disgusted, they want the perpetrator dead. If they don't feel disgust, then it's okay if he lives. It's a simple decision: thumbs up or thumbs down, like a Roman emperor at the Colosseum.

The people on TV will say that the grieving family wants "justice" and wants "closure." These are just fancy words for revenge. I am not saying that their desire for revenge is or is not justified. What I am saying is that justice and closure are not what they want, so let's stop concealing what they actually want with euphemisms.

In this country, the people want blood, as Clarence Darrow wrote in 1928:[86]

> "...the state continues to kill its victims, not so much to defend society against them ... but to appease the mob's emotions of hatred and revenge."

Politicians know what the people want, as is clearly evident from their campaign ads. They say things like, "My opponent is soft on crime. When he was a judge, he once gave a convicted sex offender a shorter sentence than the prosecutor had recommended. So vote for Hunter Lynch. He'll lock those bastards up for ever and ever." Or, "When my opponent was a judge, he once let a convicted murderer go free just because the prosecution fabricated most of the evidence against him. So vote for Ichabod Stone; he'll make sure the Constitution is used to make you more safe, not less. I'm Ichabod Stone and I approved this message."

I think you'd have to say that in this area, our democracy is working. The mob wants blood, and the lawmakers deliver. The people are being faithfully represented and their desires are accurately reflected in our laws. All of the academic debates about the efficacy and morality of capital punishment are moot.

What's more, these debates are all based on a flawed assumption—namely, that we have a well-functioning legal system. They assume we have an adversarial system of justice where both sides, prosecution and defense, fight hard, and, from this, the truth emerges. They assume that judges and attorneys are highly competent and diligent and on those extraordinarily rare occasions when they are not, we have a

---

[86] Darrow, Clarence *The Futility of the Death Penalty* The Forum, September 1928.

well-functioning appellate court system to correct the errors. They assume that expert witnesses such as coroners, medical examiners, forensic pathologists and psychologists are all highly-trained professionals who would never lie on the witness stand.

All of these assumptions are false. The prosecution has unlimited money to spend in order to get a conviction and defense lawyers have given up trying to fight back. Judges care more about ego, status, and respect than they do about justice, mercy, or the welfare of the community. With the exception of the very, very rich, nobody gets a fair trial.

If we as a society cannot create and maintain a justice system that is fair to both sides, then we do not deserve the power to execute criminals. We, as a society, focus on the crime that the criminal has committed and say, "How horrible! He doesn't deserve to live!" And that may be true. The word "deserve" is completely subjective, and reasonable people can disagree about what somebody does or does not deserve. But we never seem to look in the mirror and ask whether we deserve to be able to kill him.

The problem is us. We are not worthy of this awesome power. We are lazy. We are vain. We are dishonest. We are fat. We are greedy. We are wrathful. In short: we suck. Go walk around the food court at your local shopping mall and look around. Tell me you disagree. Watch the senate confirmation hearings for a Supreme Court nominee. Tell me you disagree.

Basically, what I'm saying is: Let him who is without sin among you cast the first stone.

Yeah, that's right: The Gospel of John, chapter eight, verse seven. I am saying the exact same thing that Jesus said. You still wanna argue with me?

"How dare you compare yourself to Jesus?"

I'm not comparing myself to Jesus. I'm comparing myself *with*[87] Jesus. And by doing so, I see that Jesus and I are saying the same thing. Me and Jee agree. Ya feel me?

---

[87] Compare: v. 1. To examine two or more objects, ideas, people, etc., in order to note similarities and differences.
Usage: the traditional rule states that COMPARE should be followed by 'to' when it points out likenesses between unlike persons or things: "She compared his handwriting to knotted string." It should be followed by 'with' when it examines two entities of the same general class for similarities or differences: "She compared his handwriting with mine."

Chapter 27: How to Fix the System

Near the end of books like this one, it is customary for the author to make suggestions and proposals, usually directed toward policy makers, for ways to improve the system. This is sensible in that there is not much point in complaining about a problem if there is no way to make it better. But, as you may have noticed, the author of this book is an inveterate cynic. So even though I am going to keep to custom, I will tell you at the outset that it is also customary for policy makers to completely ignore those suggestions.

Citizens of this fine country who are unhappy and wish to change its laws are told to "write your congressman," or "vote for political candidates who share your views." But I ask you, does that ever work? Ever? A large portion of this country would like to make abortion illegal. That is basically all they care about, and they vote exclusively for anti-abortion candidates. They've been doing so for 50 years—ever since Roe v. Wade. But abortion is still legal (for now—and the changes that have occurred since the time of writing haven't come about just by people voting. There have been hundreds of millions of right-wing religious fundamentalist dollars and scores of think-tanks working round the clock to achieve what they have). Those kids from Marjorie Stoneman Douglass High School in Florida are organizing and trying to get gun control legislation passed. I think that Florida has actually become more gun-friendly, not less, since the mass shooting at their high school. These methods of changing our laws do not seem to work.

The irony is that our government was deliberately designed to ensure that such methods fail—to thwart people who try to change the system. James Madison said so explicitly in Federalist Paper #10. He called any group of people who want to change our government or its laws a "faction," writing:

"By a faction, I understand a number of citizens, whether amounting to a majority or minority of the whole, who are united and actuated by some common impulse of passion, or interest, adverse to the right of other citizens, or to the permanent and aggregate interests of the community."

So, people who want gun control are a faction. People who oppose gun control are also a faction. People who are pro-life are a faction. People who are pro-choice are also a faction. Black Lives Matter is a faction. The Ku Klux Klan is a faction.

Madison disliked factions and touted as one of the very best features of our constitution that it would make it nearly impossible for factions to ever get what they want:

"Among the numerous advantages promised by a well-constructed Union, none deserves to be more accurately developed than its tendency to break and control the violence of factions."

How does our Constitution protect against factions? By establishing a republic, not a democracy. In a republic, the desires of any faction must be filtered through the elected representatives, which causes the faction to fizzle out:

"...the ... advantage, which a Republic has over a Democracy, in controlling the effects of factions [is that] the influence of factious leaders may kindle a flame within their particular states, but will be unable to spread a general conflagration through the other states."

That's why you can't change the system by voting for congressmen and senators who share your views. It fails because the U.S. government is designed to make it fail. This is a feature, not a bug.

Another tactic people use to affect change is peaceful protest. They march up and down the street carrying banners and chanting, "What do we want? Change! When do we want it? Now!"

Does that ever work? Supposedly, it worked for the Civil Rights movement in the 1960s. But that movement involved much more than marching and chanting. People got beaten up on bridges. People sat at lunch counters and disrupted businesses. People got arrested. People got killed. Marching alone didn't get the job done.

To be honest, I'm a little fuzzy on how, precisely, peaceful protest achieves anything. We are supposed to believe that marching up and down the street will cause our political leaders to emerge from the darkness of their hidebound ways into the resplendent light of truth and then change our laws for the better? That seems like a fairy tale. Why wouldn't they just say, "Look at all those idiots walking up and down the street and clogging up traffic. I sure am glad I'm not one of them?" In fact, that is essentially what happened during the Occupy Wall Street protests. The traders and bankers of Goldman Sachs looked down at the protesters from the windows of their corporate skyscraper and laughed. No bankers were ever punished for the financial collapse of 2008.[88]

So, how do you change the government? How do you change the laws? You change the government with money.

---

[88] Actually, that's hyperbole. One Credit Suisse trader, Kareem Serageldin, was sentenced to 30 months for fraudulently inflating the prices of subprime mortgage-backed securities. Twenty trillion dollars in losses; one Egyptian guy got two and a half years.

Wall Street bankers, oil, coal, and pharmaceutical executives all seem to be able to shape the laws to their advantage. Do they achieve this by voting for like-minded political candidates? Do they achieve this through peaceful protest? No. They achieve it by buying politicians. This is done with campaign contributions and lobbying. How much money do they spend to make this work? I'm not sure—billions, maybe? Hundreds of millions at the very least. It's out of my price range, I'm sure about that.

It seems to me that there is only one place where defendants can apply any real pressure: on defense attorneys. Prosecutors and judges are part of the government. They are elected. Their salaries are paid by taxpayers. So they are untouchable. But defense attorneys are paid by defendants. (Not public defenders. They are paid by the state. But defense attorneys in private practice get their money from their clients.) Defendants get to talk directly to the defense attorneys. Their families can call the defense attorneys at their offices or text them or e-mail them.

Defense attorneys, quite simply, are not doing their jobs. They are not fighting hard against prosecutors. At trial, they roll over and play dead and hope the prosecutor throws them a doggy biscuit once in a while. They don't stand up to intimidation by judges. They don't work hard. They don't really know the law. The client should not have to pay for the attorney's time researching the law. The attorney is supposed to be an expert at the law already. That is why the client hired the attorney: for his knowledge of and expertise in the law.

I see three ways that defendants can try to improve the system. I can't guarantee that they will work, but they seem to me like the most promising places to start.

(1) Force the crappiest defense attorneys out of the system.

This requires the ability to distinguish the good attorneys from the bad ones.

Defendants need to be able to rate and review their lawyers' performances and then post these reviews on the internet for others to read and learn from - sort of a Rotten Tomatoes or Yelp for defense attorneys. It is important that only actual defendants be allowed to post reviews. We don't want trolls coming in and artificially inflating or deflating the ratings. Both defendants who won and defendants who lost should post reviews so that prospective clients can get a complete picture of a lawyer's performance over a wide range of cases.

I'm sure there could be counterarguments about how such a system could induce lawyers to refuse difficult clients and only accept slam-dunk cases in order to raise their ratings. Such arguments are bogus. The future is too hard to predict, especially when dealing with human behavior. In this particular case, we don't know if the assigned cause would be of sufficient strength to actually cause the alleged bad outcome.

Counterarguments of the form, "We shouldn't try X because Y might happen" always seem to come from people who are very happy with the status quo and therefore resistant to any change. Before I believe such an argument, I like to see some actual evidence that change X causes outcome Y. Also, if X does cause Y, will it really make the system worse? The system is really bad right now. Currently, defense lawyers lie to their clients until they get all the money they can from them and then try to convince them to take a plea, or, if they end up going to trial, they put in as little work as possible and don't defend their clients at all. If the criminal justice system were a finely tuned mechanism for punishing the guilty and exonerating the innocent, then I could understand why maybe you would not want to tamper with it. But it's not. It is an unfair piece of junk that only serves the interests of lawyers. So let's try a few changes and see what happens.

(2) Force the remaining defense attorneys to work harder, make better decisions, and lie less.

Forcing defense attorneys to make better decisions, work harder, and tell fewer lies requires educating defendants. Improvements to the system can be achieved by a series of small and correct choices by defendants. By choosing to read this book, you have already made one correct choice. Defendants should become able to make better plea bargain decisions, understand sentencing guidelines in order to fight back when they are overcharged, notice when their attorney fails to object, make the attorney tell the jury clearly that the defendant is innocent, prevent the attorney from waiving his client's rights, etc.

(3) Increase transparency by collecting statistics and making them easily accessible to defendants.

There are many simple statistics that currently are either hidden from defendants or not collected at all. The following is a preliminary list of basic stats that would be helpful.

A. Of defendants who go to trial, what percent win, what percent lose? Break this down by state, county, judge, and crime. If a defendant could see that 28 out of the last 29 murder trials in his county resulted in a guilty verdict, maybe he would be more likely to accept the prosecution's plea offer and save his family a lot of money and stress.

B. What have the defendant's lawyer's results been? How many wins? How many losses? How many plea deals? Defendants are flying blind when it comes to evaluating and choosing defense attorneys.

C. Of defendants who take the stand and testify in their own defense, what percent win? What percent lose? If it turns out to be the case that defendants who testify achieve significantly better results than defendants who don't testify, it would be nice to know that.

D. What percent of appeals achieve any kind of victory? What is your appellate lawyer's record? How many appeals has he won? How many has he lost?

All of these should be collected and made easily accessible to the public. Sunlight is the best disinfectant. It's a cliche, but it's true. People are completely unaware of how biased the system has become and how badly defense attorneys are defending their clients. Let's get the information out there where everybody can see it.

Chapter 28: Conclusion

You've been arrested and you've been indicted. You are now playing a game that you cannot win. You have entered a carnival funhouse with no lights other than the flashlights held by the carnies whom you should not trust. They are all lying to you: the prosecutor, the judge, and even your own lawyer whom you have paid to help you—*especially* your own lawyer—because the prosecutor and the judge speak to you only through him.

I told you up front that the most prudent course is to accept the plea deal that they offer you. I stand by that, but to those of you who still intend to fight, I salute you. Not only do I salute you, but I have provided you with advanced knowledge of many of the lies that will surely be told to you as you proceed through your journey.

Perhaps you are still skeptical of my characterization of the criminal justice system. Can it really be as bad as I say? Can the judge, prosecutor, and defense attorney really all be colluding against the defendant? That just sounds like too big a conspiracy to keep secret. There are thousands of judges and tens of thousands of lawyers and millions of people being arrested and charged with crimes. If the prosecutors were really winning 99 percent of the time and defense attorneys were taking dives when they had winning cases, surely people would have found out about all this by now. People who have been screwed over by their lawyers would be shouting it from the rooftops. There would be "good" defense attorneys pointing fingers at the "bad" defense attorneys, if for no other reason than to get more business. And if a judge found out about all the cheating that was going on, boy, oh boy, he'd have those dirty defense lawyers disbarred, wouldn't he? And judges can't really cheat because they have to provide reasons in writing for all of their decisions, which may then be reviewed by appellate courts. Those appellate court judges would surely keep the lower court judges in line.

Wouldn't they?

In fact, people who've been screwed over by their lawyers *are* shouting it from the rooftops: the rooftops of their prisons. When you get screwed over by a criminal defense lawyer, you go to prison. And when you yell from the rooftops of a prison, nobody hears you. That's how the medical profession was able to survive for hundreds of years when it was harming the patients more than it helped: it buried all of its failures, and its successes lived to tell the world how much the doctor had helped them.

Maybe you're also wondering who planned this whole thing. Who got all the prosecutors and defense attorneys to agree that this was the way things were going to work? This sort of thinking is treacherous. Many natural and social systems behave in ways that fool people into believing that there must be some malign human intelligence guiding things from behind the curtain.

Never forget that money is the lifeblood of the criminal justice system. Nobody denies this. Even the staunchest apologists admit it. They just say it is a necessary evil and we shouldn't worry too much about it. Lawyers all have bills to pay. They all borrowed money to go to law school.

Any system that involves money will without doubt be influenced and shaped by market forces. Nobody denies this, either. The economist Adam Smith, writing in 1776, called this influence "the invisible hand."[89] He wrote of

---

[89] I find it peculiar that if you say "conspiracy theory" everyone will laugh at you and say "Don't be ridiculous," whereas if you say "Invisible Hand" everybody nods their head approvingly and willingly accepts this as a perfectly believable explanation. Invisible hands are imaginary, like magic wands. Conspiracies are real. Brutus and Cassius conspired to murder Caesar.

workers and consumers, but it applies to lawyers just as well. *"...he intends only his own gain, and he is in this, as in many other cases, led by an invisible hand to promote and end which was no part of his intention."* This is what tricks people into believing that there must be some force acting behind the scenes: the fact that the "end" that obtains was not intended by any of the actors in the system.

The criminal justice system is corruptible in the same ways that all markets are corruptible. Money is the greatest conspiracy, we are all addicted to it and there is nowhere to hide from it. Corruption does not require a conspiracy or a hidden cabal or any kind of planning committee. It just requires money.

Defense lawyers, prosecutors, and judges are all acting in their self-interest, subject to the incentives and constraints of their business. They want to make as much money as possible for as little work as possible. They want to be promoted. They want to be liked and respected by their colleagues. Each lawyer considers, as he makes every important decision, the reactions he anticipates from his peers and his superiors whom he hopes to impress.

Consider the following law of markets: if three people are competing, eventually two of them will join together and gang up on the third. It is inevitable. This has now happened in the legal system. The prosecutors and judges have joined forces and teamed up against the defense attorneys. And the result has been that prosecutors all have conviction rates well north of 90 percent.

Think about how high that is. the greatest coach in NFL history, Bill Belichick, has a winning percentage nowhere near that high. And he cheats! He's been caught cheating.

People argue over who is the greatest basketball player of all time. Is it Michael Jordan? Is it Lebron James? Each of these men has played basketball for almost their whole lives. They have each, in their lives, taken hundreds of thousands of practice free throws. Jordan was an 83 percent free throw shooter for his career. Lebron James has only managed 73 percent. Both of these gods of the NBA pantheon pale in comparison to a mid-career assistant prosecutor from Oshkosh, Wisconsin.

What is the mechanism that would prevent collusion and corruption in the criminal justice system from happening? Lawyers and judges police themselves. There is no outside accountability. This leads to corruption. It is inevitable.

As for preventing the corruption from being exposed, it's much easier than you'd think. In major league baseball, for an entire decade, players were suddenly hitting 50 percent more home runs and their heads were growing two hat sizes, yet most people refused to believe that they were taking steroids. Then some players, e.g., Jose Canseco, came forward and said, "Everybody is taking steroids. I've witnessed it with my own eyes. I've personally stuck the needle in many players' asses." Still, nobody believed him. He was ridiculed and reviled. They said "Oh, he's just saying that because he got caught taking steroids. It's just sour grapes." And on it went. Then, by the end of the decade, it became clear that all the big home run hitters were taking steroids: Bonds, Sosa, McGwire, Rodriguez, and many others.

The same basic pattern has occurred in professional cycling, mortgage fraud, insider trading, and government corruption coverups. Usually, it is the whistleblowers who really suffer, not the cheaters at the top of the pyramid.

So, believe me when I tell you that you cannot trust your lawyer; you cannot trust the prosecutors; and you cannot trust the judge. You're going to have to work hard to learn the truth, and you need the truth, for the truth shall set you free.

Afterword

If you have reached this page, you have looked through the looking glass. I am grateful to you for reading the book. This book was written by a person who has been through the system to a person who is about to. If the information presented in this book was useful to you, I hope you will consider taking any or all of the following actions:

1. The most effective thing you can do now is to return to Amazon and leave a rating and a brief review. This is not a request for praise. Amazon's algorithms rely on review volume to determine visibility. A review increases the statistical likelihood that this book will appear in the search results of other people.

2. If you know others who are operating under the standard illusions about how the justice system works, feel free to mention is book to them. You do not need to convince them of anything or argue a position. The text speaks for itself. But as a lone inmate inside a penitentiary, it is nearly impossible for me to promote this message without your help.

3. The people who would most benefit from reading this book are those that have just been arrested and have never been through the system before. If you would give a copy of the book to someone in jail, or donate a copy to your local county jail, or even just donate a copy to your local public library, that would be a good thing.

Yours with gratitude and respect,

Daniel

243

www.ingramcontent.com/pod-product-compliance
Lightning Source LLC
Chambersburg PA
CBHW071552210326
41597CB00019B/3204